Shire County Guide 37

SUFFOLK

Tim Buxbaum

Shire Publications Ltd

2

Published in 1996 by Shire Publications Ltd, Cromwell House, Church Street, Princes Risborough, Buckinghamshire HP27 9AA, UK.
Copyright © 1996 by Tim Buxbaum. First published 1996. Shire County Guide 37. ISBN 0 7478 0319 6.
Tim Buxbaum is hereby identified as the author of this work in accordance with section 77 of the Copyright, Designs and Patents Act 1988.

Printed in Great Britain by CIT Printing Services, Press Buildings, Merlins Bridge, Haverfordwest, Dyfed SA61 1XF.

British Library Cataloguing in Publication Data: Buxbaum, Tim. Suffolk. - (Shire County Guide ; 37) 1. Suffolk (England) - Guidebooks I. Title 914.2'64'04859 ISBN 0747803196

Acknowledgements

Photographs are acknowledged as follows: Gainsborough Silk Weaving Company, page 115; Dona Haycraft, page 3; Kentwell Hall, page 93 (top); Cadbury Lamb, pages 18, 21, 25, 29, 31, 43 (both), 44 (bottom), 45, 50, 63, 76, 87, 90, 93 (bottom), 99, 101, 109, 117, 121; Mechanical Music Museum Trust (photograph by Terence J. Burchett), page 104; National Horseracing Museum (photograph by Laurie Morton), page 107; St Edmundsbury Borough Council/West Stow Anglo-Saxon Village Trust, page 96. All other photographs are by the author, Tim Buxbaum.

The map on pages 4 and 5 is by Robert Dizon, using Ordnance Survey material. The National Grid References in the text are included by permission of the Controller of Her Majesty's Stationery Office.

Ordnance Survey grid references

Although information on how to reach most of the places described in this book by car is given in the text, National Grid References are also included in many instances, particularly for the harder-to-find places in chapters 3, 5 and 9, for the benefit of those readers who have the Ordnance Survey 1:50,000 Landranger maps of the area. The references are stated as a Landranger sheet number followed by the 100 km National Grid square and the six-figure reference.

To locate a site by means of the grid references, proceed as in the following example: Leiston Abbey (OS 156: TM 444642). Take the OS Landranger map sheet 156 ('Saxmundham, Aldeburgh and surrounding area'). The grid numbers are printed in blue around the edges of the map. In more recently produced maps these numbers are repeated at 10 km intervals throughout the map, so that it is not necessary to open it out completely.) Read off these numbers from the left along the top edge of the map until you come to 44, denoting a vertical grid line, then estimate four-tenths of the distance to vertical line 45 and envisage an imaginary vertical grid line 44.4 at this point. Next look at the grid numbers at one side of the map (either side will do) and read *upwards* until you find the horizontal grid line 64. Estimate two tenths of the distance to the next horizontal line above (i.e. 65), and so envisage an imaginary horizontal line across the map at 64.2. Follow this imaginary line across the map until it crosses the imaginary vertical line 44.4. At the intersection of these two lines you will find Leiston Abbey.

The Ordnance Survey Landranger maps which cover Suffolk are sheets 134, 143, 144, 154, 155, 156 and 169. A very small area of the county is found on map 168.

Cover: *The Moot Hall, Aldeburgh. (Photograph by Cadbury Lamb.)*

Contents

Blackthorpe Barn at Rougham was built c.1550.

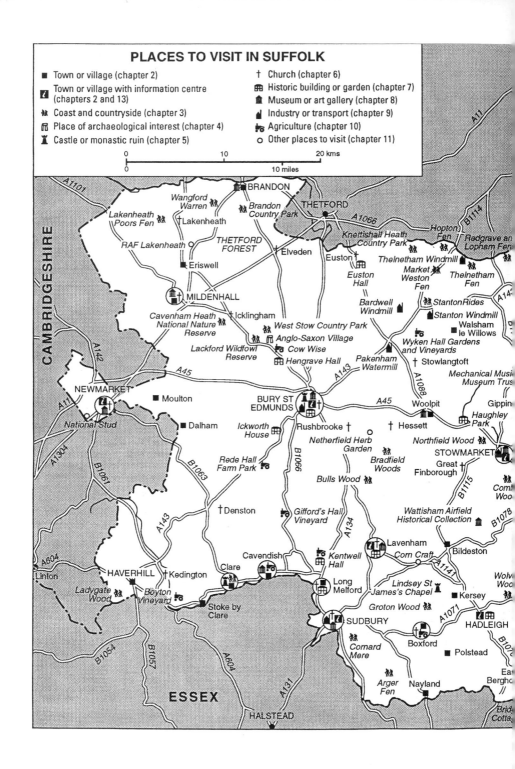

PLACES TO VISIT IN SUFFOLK

- ■ Town or village (chapter 2)
- *i* Town or village with information centre (chapters 2 and 13)
- ⚲ Coast and countryside (chapter 3)
- ⬚ Place of archaeological interest (chapter 4)
- ⚊ Castle or monastic ruin (chapter 5)

- † Church (chapter 6)
- ⊞ Historic building or garden (chapter 7)
- ⬛ Museum or art gallery (chapter 8)
- ◢ Industry or transport (chapter 9)
- ⛏ Agriculture (chapter 10)
- o Other places to visit (chapter 11)

0 ———— 10 ———— 20 kms
0 ———— 10 miles

CAMBRIDGESHIRE

A1101

A11

B1114

BRANDON
Wangford Warren ⚲
Brandon Country Park
THETFORD
A1066
Lakenheath Poors Fen ⚲
† Lakenheath
Hopton Fen
Knettishall Heath Country Park ⚲
Redgrave an Lopham Fen
RAF Lakenheath O
THETFORD FOREST
† Elveden
Euston †
Thelnetham Windmill
Eriswell ■
Euston Hall
Market Weston ⚲ Fen
Thelnetham Fen
A14
MILDENHALL
Bardwell Windmill
Stanton Rides ⚲
Stanton Windmill
Cavenham Heath National Nature Reserve ⚲
† Icklingham
West Stow Country Park
Walsham le Willows ■
Lackford Wildfowl Reserve
Anglo-Saxon Village
⛏ Cow Wise
Wyken Hall Gardens and Vineyards
Hengrave Hall ⊞
Pakenham Watermill
† Stowlangtoft
A143
A1088
Mechanical Music Museum Trus
NEWMARKET
A142
A45
BURY ST EDMUNDS
A45
Woolpit ■
Gippin
Haughley Park ⊞
Moulton ■
National Stud
A11
A1304
Dalham ■
Ickworth House ⊞
Rushbrooke †
† Hessett
Northfield Wood ⚲
STOWMARKET
B1061
Netherfield Herb Garden o
Bradfield Woods ⚲
Great Finborough †
Com Woo
A143
B1063
Rede Hall Farm Park ⛏
B1066
Bulls Wood ⚲
Wattisham Airfield Historical Collection ⬛
B1078
† Denston
Gifford's Hall Vineyard
A134
Lavenham
Corn Craft
Bildeston ■
A1141
HAVERHILL
† Kedington
Clare
Cavendish
⛏ Kentwell Hall ⊞
Lindsey St James's Chapel ⚊
Kersey ■
Wolv Woo
Ladygate Wood ⚲
Boyton Vineyard ⛏
Stoke by Clare
Long Melford
Groton Wood ⚲
A1071
HADLEIGH
Linton
A604
SUDBURY
Boxford †
Polstead ■
B1054
B1057
A604
A131
Cornard Mere ⚲
Arger Fen ⚲
Nayland
Eas Bergho
Brid Cotta

ESSEX

HALSTEAD

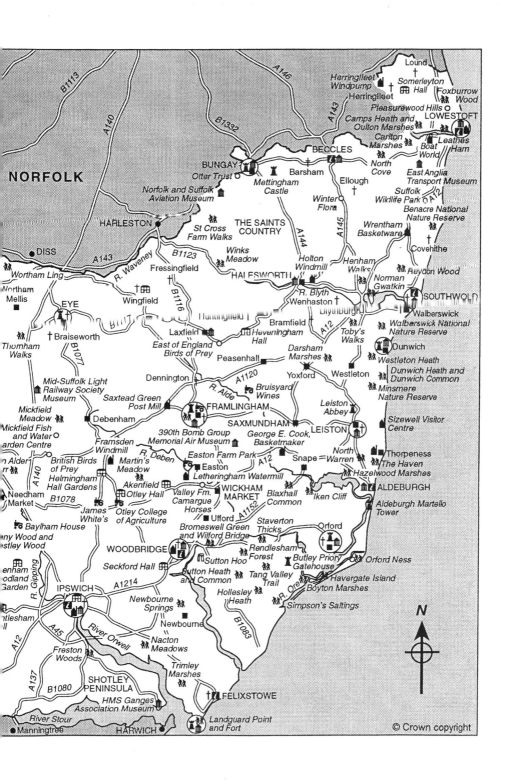

Preface

Welcome to the Shire County Guide to Suffolk, one of over thirty such books, written and designed to enable you to organise your time in the county well.

The Shire County Guides fill the need for a compact, accurate and thorough guide to each county so that visitors can plan a half-day excursion or a whole week's stay to best advantage. Residents, too, will find the guides a handy and reliable reference to the places of interest in their area.

Travelling British roads can be time consuming, and the County Guides will ensure that you need not inadvertently miss any interesting feature in a locality, that you do not accidentally bypass a new museum or an outstanding church, that you can find an attractive place to picnic, and that you will appreciate the history and the buildings of the towns or villages in which you stop.

This book has been arranged in special interest chapters, such as the coast and countryside, castles and monastic ruins, and museums and art galleries, and all these places of interest are located on the map on pages 4-5. Use the map either for an overview to decide which area has most to interest you, or to help you enjoy your immediate neighbourhood. Then refer to the nearest town or village in chapter 2 to see, at a glance, what special features or attractions each community contains or is near. The subsequent chapters enable readers with a particular interest to find immediately those places of importance to them, while the cross-referencing under 'Suffolk Towns and Villages' assists readers with wider tastes to select how best to spend their time.

Details of opening dates of the attractions described in this book are included for the guidance of readers and were believed to be correct at the time of writing. However, they are liable to subsequent alteration and to avoid disappointment they should be checked before setting out on a visit, by telephoning either the attraction itself or one of the tourist information centres listed in chapter 13.

Fishing boats on the shingle beach at Aldeburgh.

1

Introduction

Suffolk occupies the middle part of the bulge of East Anglia and its boundaries are distinct. To the east, against hard shingly shores, the North Sea erodes and accretes: pewter-coloured, bleak and inspiring, white-flecked or deceptively blue, it has fought Suffolk for centuries. There are lighthouses and estuaries, the cries of gulls, fishermen, scant harbours and a history of smuggling. Lowestoft Ness is England's most easterly point. Inland, saltmarsh and sandy heaths give way to rich farmland.

To the north, between Bury St Edmunds and Newmarket, there are tracts of forest and heathy Breckland bordered to Norfolk by the marshy rivers Waveney and Little Ouse. Southern Suffolk comprises rolling hills and valleys – a softer, prettier landscape, especially around the river Stour, where from the eighteenth century improving transport generated large country houses. The western boundary with Cambridgeshire is partly defined by the Devil's Dyke, a 7 miles (11 km) long earthwork in chalky downland which soon becomes fen; for years these features and natural forest deflected potential incomers.

Modern Suffolk is predominantly rural and agricultural with shallow river valleys, woodland and rolling clay lands growing wheat, barley, sugar beet, rape and linseed. Camden's *Britannia*, published in Latin in 1586, described the county as 'full of havens of a fat and fertile soil' with 'most rich and goodly cornfields'. Centuries later, John Constable eulogised 'its gentle declivities, its luxuriant meadow flats sprinkled with flocks and herds, its well cultivated uplands, its woods and rivers, with numerous scattered villages and churches, farms and picturesque cottages'. Today's landscape retains a gentle subtle beauty which away from the towns unfolds under vast skies, enhanced by a special mutable quality of light, most marked near the coast. The climate is generally moderate and dry.

Although Suffolk is less than a hundred miles from London, through traffic concentrates on the ports and principal roads such as the A12 from London and the A14 to the Midlands. Many country areas, with their tiny roads, remain independent and tranquil, apparently resisting incoming 'furriners'. Yet the county has not been remote; after King Edmund's martyrdom in AD 869 Bury St Edmunds Abbey attracted pilgrims from all over Christendom. In 1214, before that abbey's high altar, Cardinal Langton and twenty-five English barons swore to persuade King John to accept Magna Carta. Through Cromwell's Civil War the county supported the Parliamentarians. Today, Suffolk is famous for the Aldeburgh Music Festival, Snape Maltings and the port of Felixstowe. Many people come to enjoy its natural beauty.

Suffolk was first recorded as a county in 1044 when it was feudally split between Bury St Edmunds Abbey and Ely; it was later controlled by local families such as the de la Poles and the Bigods. Later still, parliamentary constituencies were rearranged under the 1832 Reform Act, which officially recognised the decline since the middle ages of such boroughs such as Eye, Sudbury, Dunwich and Aldeburgh. East and West Suffolk County Councils were set up in 1888, to be merged in 1974 into Suffolk County Council with six administrative districts. The county's overall area is 380,000 hectares or 1500 square miles and the 1991 population census recorded 649,600 inhabitants. Between 1961 and 1971 the population increased by 18 per cent.

Medieval Suffolk's great wealth came from textiles (produced before the industrial revolution took production north) and from port industries, which suffered as the ports silted up. By 1700 Suffolk was the twelfth poorest county in England. From then on, the coun-

Typical 'flushwork' between the carvings on St Mary's church, Woodbridge.

ty's economy was tied to agriculture, its economic success reflecting the construction of navigable waterways and railways, the Napoleonic Wars, the Corn Laws, the mechanisation of farming and the Common Agricultural Policy. Since the 1960s Suffolk's economy has diversified and grown quickly, encouraged by proximity to Europe and many tourist attractions. The principal towns are Ipswich and Bury St Edmunds, followed by the ports of Felixstowe and Lowestoft.

Suffolk people are traditionally shrewd, conservative and difficult to hurry. Much local folklore relates to smugglers and ghosts. For centuries smuggling was rife all down the coast, carried out by individuals and large armed gangs on horseback who specialised in tea or liquor. Many towns had at least one house where the smugglers' lookout displayed an ornamental cat in the window as a warning that customs officers were expected.

Suffolk has minimal building stone. Chalk and softer clunch were quarried inland, sedimentary Coralline Crag and ironstone nearer the sea. Mudstone Septaria was taken from estuarine riverbanks – much of Orford Castle is made of it – and church towers were raised in all sorts of materials including sarsens deposited by glaciers. Dressed stone in Suffolk is usually limestone imported ingeniously from the East Midlands or France.

The chalk beds provided flints which were either used whole as smooth round stones or deliberately split or knapped into hard shiny fragments laid in lime mortar. Flint walls with brick dressings are typical; the more imposing churches go further, combining cream limestone with black-grey flints patterned into chequerboards, lozenges or cinquefoils – an art called 'flushwork'.

Buildings with softer lines resulted from the widespread use of sun-dried clay mixed with straw to form building blocks of 'clay lump'. The result is often faced with lime plaster and colourwashed – most popular in villages on the heavier soils of High Suffolk.

Suffolk has an excellent heritage of timber construction, including historic barns, pubs, houses, windmills and church roofs, all utilising the natural shape of the wood and jointed without nails. Oak was pre-eminent, readily carved when green, weathering to a lovely silver grey and sometimes distorting dramatically to give wildly leaning walls. The size and proximity of the constructional studs indicated prestige, the gaps between being infilled with daub and wattle, often later replaced with brick nogging, plaster and colourwash. Such construction developed a particular vocabulary revelling in dragonbeams, bressumers, windbracing, jetting and associated joints and carvings. The complex development of timber-framed construction is well illustrated in cloth towns like Lavenham and Long Melford, reflecting a peak of wealth in the early sixteenth century.

Many Elizabethan buildings were elaborately detailed with carved porches and bargeboards, pargeting, complex windows with leaded lights and overhanging or jetted first floors. From the later seventeenth century such features were seen as archaic, so ground-floor walls were moved outwards and new walls built neatly vertical to give fashionable flush frontages of brick punctuated with pediments, porticoes and sash windows.

The fine brickwork of Suffolk, begun in Roman times, was revived in medieval churches and barns. Bricks were locally burned or shipped in as ballast for exported cloth. The results were rendered and lined to imitate stone or expressed in shaped mullions and arcading. Abundant local clay and a spate of rebuilding following town fires increased Suffolk's brick production during the seventeenth century, spreading down the social scale from grand houses to cottages, providing fireproof chimneys and solid walls. Dark header bricks were used to pick out geometric patterns; Dutch influence brought curved gables. The Georgians preferred restrained façades, fashionably refacing older buildings and enjoying serpentine crinkle-crankle walls. The Victorians fired red, grey and yellow local clays and distributed them on the new railways; often the harder whites were used to edge red-brick compositions. Brickworks flourished all over Suffolk: Somerleyton bricks built Liverpool Street station in London, Sudbury bricks the Royal Albert Hall. The industry declined so that by the 1980s only three brickworks were left.

There are no naturally occurring slates for miles around Suffolk and, for roofing, flat pegtiles and curved pantiles were imported or fired locally, including shiny black salt glazed pantiles which glisten in the sun. Before tiles were easily available, roofs were thatched in longstraw, from wheat, with hazel rodding and a simple flush ridge. This traditional craft suffered from changing agricultural practice, including combine harvesters and new crops, but water reed and sedge remain popular near the reedbeds. Combed wheat reed or Devon reed, with its close-cropped moulded appearance, is alien to Suffolk.

Suffolk's towns and villages are full of buildings reflecting centuries of use of these materials – of mellow brickwork and complementary colourwashed frontages carrying windows on the outside faces of their walls. Often there seems to be much more wall than window, the wall sometimes being patterned with applied decoration called pargeting, best seen at the Ancient House in Ipswich or in Clare. Internally, similar decoration has produced some wonderful plaster ceilings, as at Hintlesham Hall.

A flint pebble boundary wall with brick buttresses and coping at Southwold.

2
Suffolk towns and villages

Suffolk comprises a few large towns and over four hundred villages, many with populations of five hundred or less. A high proportion of these existed at Domesday (1086). Their names give clues to their histories. Thus Oakley, Occold and Eyke all derive from the old Scandinavian for oak, whilst village subdivision is reflected in 'Magna' and 'Parva' (at Thornham), or 'Inferior' and 'Superior' (at Rickinghall). Bradfield Combust may relate to fire-raising in the Peasants' Revolt.

There are scores of 'Greens' and 'Tyes', formed after 1300 for public grazing, some relating to sites of plague or fire. Most have been modified, subdivided, joined up or built over, given meaningful names like Workhouse Green, Maypole Green and Frizzeler's Green. The eleven greens at Wickhambrook or the nine at Cockfield probably recall early cultivation of the forested clay land, when clearings for farms and manors were gradually extended, resulting in the present scattering of hamlets, pubs and churches across the landscape.

As common land was enclosed, so were many traditional greens destroyed. Nathaniel Bloomfield's 'Elegy on the Enclosure of Honington Green' lamented its demise in 1801: 'In all seasons the Green we lov'd most, Because on the Green we were free.' A few unenclosed and flower-studded greens remain yet, at Chippenhall, Wortham and Mellis, the last so large it is crossed by the railway.

Through the middle ages, encouraged by trade, towns grew, markets were chartered and success brought prestige and a larger church. Across Suffolk, many settlements prospered from the cloth industry yet remained static thereafter, surviving as picturesque villages. Their medieval origins are visible through a collage of brickwork and colourwash, of soft waviness and irregularity, of broad main streets leading out to open countryside past an easy mixture of unselfconscious cottages and civic buildings.

The population figures given in this chapter are derived from the 1992 County Council Census.

Aldeburgh
OS 156: TM 465565. Population 2700.
Early closing Wednesday.

Tudor prosperity declined as two harbours silted up and half the lower town disappeared under the sea. Partly isolated by a wide curve of the well-sailed river Alde, Aldeburgh's individual character is nowadays crowded and delightful in summer, desolate in winter. Its famous residents have included George Crabbe, Elizabeth Garrett Anderson and Benjamin Britten. Crag Path is the seafront promenade to a good pebble beach; overlooking it are exuberant and eclectic houses with colourful balconies and secure floodboards,

including Strafford House, minuscule Fantasia and two lookout towers built for rival salvage firms, the Up-Towners and the Down-Towners. There is also the lifeboat station, open to the public, which houses a tractor-launched boat. Facing it is Jubilee Hall, where the Aldeburgh Festival began. At one end of Crag Path stands The Old Mill House, converted to a residence in 1902 by a monk who left holy orders for a Scandinavian wife. Towards the other end is grassy Moot Green with a model boating pond guarded by the statue of a faithful small dog.

Years ago, several streets ran parallel with Crag Path. Now only two remain: narrow

Crabbe Street and the broad High Street with its mock-Tudor cinema, Georgian shopfronts, pebble-built cottages, old customs house and small sheltered footpaths like Neptune Alley. Behind High Street the cliff rises up to the residential upper town, best reached via the Town Steps, with good rooftop views and seascapes. The road rises steeply to the parish church, a former seamark, wherein stained glass by John Piper pays tribute to Britten; ship auctions once took place in the nave. Further south, an unusual water tower, in Park Road, and substantial Arts and Crafts houses survey open marshland.

Just south of the town, by the yacht clubs, is the site of the former fishing and shipbuilding village of Slaughden, now completely below the sea.

The renowned Aldeburgh Music Festival takes place annually and there is a summer carnival.

Aldeburgh Martello Tower, page 73; **Moot Hall Museum**, page 102.

In Aldeburgh churchyard is this memorial to lifeboatmen lost at sea.

In the locality: The Haven, page 64; Hazelwood Marshes, page 64; the Long Shop Museum, page 106; North Warren, page 67; Orford Ness, pages 67 and 122; Suffolk Heritage Coast Path, page 68; and church at Leiston, page 90.

Aldham
Wolves Wood, page 69.

Ashbocking
James White's Apple Juice and Cider Company, page 120.

Assington
See Newbourne, page 38.

Bardwell
Bardwell Windmill, page 114.

Barking
Bonny Wood, page 61.

Barsham
Church of Holy Trinity, page 80.

Baylham
Baylham House Rare Breeds Farm, page 120.

Beccles
OS 134, 156: TM 425905. Population 9650.
Early closing Wednesday; market day Friday.

Beccles stands above fenland reclaimed from the river Waveney. Its streets have Viking names such as Saltgate, Smallgate and Sheepgate ('gate' being derived from Scandinavian *gade*, a street). In 1086 the town was still a sea port, administered from Bury St Edmunds Abbey in return for 60,000 herrings a year. Five hundred years later the townspeople retained the common land of Beccles marshes under a royal charter granted by Elizabeth I. Four disastrous fires followed in the seventeenth century but these promoted good new buildings; notable houses include Roos Hall (Barsham Road), Waveney House (Puddingmoor) and St Peter's House (Old Market).

Beccles is an attractive market town. Beside the fine St Michael's church stands its

The view down Northgate, Beccles, with its narrow frontages and Dutch gables.

detached dominant bell-tower built in stone in 1547, burnt in 1586, and now displaying on its walls a 1795 penny used, symbolically, to buy it for the townspeople in 1972. Nearby, the medieval New Market leads down Ballygate (i.e. the street leading to the Bailey) past elegantly pedimented Georgian houses. Opposite Hungate Lane, Stepping Hill drops to the river, which was once full of sailing wherries; now there are boatbuilders and pleasure craft. The road returns up Puddingmoor (or 'frog moor'), past Church Score, one of many 'scores' or streets where herrings were landed a thousand years ago, and into the Saxon Old Market, now a bus station. From here, parallel with the river and leading to the Quay, Northgate is full of narrow-fronted old houses, many with Dutch gables.

Legend has it that on 31st August each year, on a bend in the river, one can hear echoes of the pipes that once rid the town of rats in a dubious pact involving three local witches. Beccles Fair is held on St Peter's Day, in late June. Boats for the Broads can be hired from Beccles Quay.

Beccles and District Museum, page 102; **William Clowes Print Museum**, page 102.

In the locality: Bigod Way, page 61; East Anglia Transport Museum, page 106; North Cove, page 66; Winter Flora, page 123; and churches at Barsham with Shipmeadow, page 80; and Ellough, page 82.

Benacre

Benacre National Nature Reserve, page 61.

Bildeston

OS 155: TL 993495. Population 880.

A remote church on high ground marks the exposed site of the original village, which moved in the thirteenth century to take trade from the nearby Stowmarket to Hadleigh road. The town's market was chartered in 1264 and by 1520 Bildeston was an important centre for blue cloth.

The pleasing town square is surrounded by generous colourwashed frontages and a fine Georgian brick house; at its centre is a flamboyant weathervaned clock-tower, built in 1864. Adjacent Duke Street returns to the square along Chapel Street in a U shape full of timbered and plastered buildings, the best being Levells Hall. The surrounding streets are full of character, including earth walls, refronted houses, interesting pubs and the chapel built in 1731, rebuilt in 1844.

In the locality: Corn Craft, page 122; Wattisham Airfield Historical Collection, page 109.

Blaxhall
Blaxhall Common, page 61.

Blythburgh
Church of the Holy Trinity, page 80; Norman Gwatkin, page 66; Toby's Walks, page 69.

Boxford
OS 155: TL 963405. Population 1280.
An attractive village in the steep valley of the narrow river Box, Boxford prospered from cloth production and later, with Huguenot skills, from glovemaking and dressing deer skins. There are fine colourwashed frontages near St Mary's church, whence an iron bridge crosses the little river into Broad Street past a white brick fire-engine shelter dated 1828. Here are many lovely doorcases, Georgian façades and exposed timbers, particularly in Butcher's Lane. Swan Street exhibits some architectural gems, ranging in style through Georgian, Gothick and Arts and Crafts, with splendid pargeting and even some concrete Airey houses.

Church of St Mary, page 80; **Copella Fruit Juices Ltd**, page 120.

In the locality: Groton Wood, page 64; Lindsey St James's Chapel, page 77.

Boyton
Boyton Marshes, page 62.

Braiseworth
Church of St Mary, page 80.

Bramfield
Church of St Andrew, page 80.

Brandon
OS 144: TL 784865. Population 8220.
Brandon lies at the centre of Breckland on an ancient site settled by the Iceni tribe on a crossing of the Little Ouse. Its market was chartered in 1319 and it grew steadily. There is abundant local flint, used in many older and a few new buildings, providing walls of knobbly whole blue flints quoined in brick, or knapped into panels of glossy neat black squares, or used as irregular sparkling fragments in a range of greys.

Brandon was once the centre of flint knapping, providing decorative building materials and also gunflints for firearms from early flintlocks onwards. During the Napoleonic Wars two hundred flint knappers were employed in Brandon, each producing up to three hundred gunflints an hour, each gunflint reckoned to be good for five hundred shots. Production continued on a much smaller scale until the 1930s, with a late revival during the Abyssinian War against Italy.

Breckland also produced copious quantities of rabbits, introduced by the Normans, who farmed them for fur and meat. Their numbers increased from 1370 as medieval warrens were licensed, taxed and fortified with warren lodges. Modern maps of Breckland show dozens of 'Warrens', including Lakenheath Warren, probably the largest and oldest in Britain, dating from 1251; it belonged for six hundred years to the Bishops of Ely. Nearby Eriswell Warren supplied some 25,000 rabbits a year for food during the Napoleonic Wars; by then the warrens were protected with turf banks and gorse. Around 1850, Brandon became a main supplier to the British fur industry and rabbit pelts went to local felt factories like Lingwood's, still visible from the pollarded lime-tree footpath of Victoria Avenue, to be made into hats. The rabbit carcasses went to dining tables in London.

There has been considerable post-war expansion of Brandon and its surroundings because of Anglo-American military activities.

Brandon Country Park, page 62; **Brandon Heritage Centre**, page 102.

In the locality: Lakenheath Poors Fen, page 65; RAF Lakenheath, page 123; Wangford Warren, page 69; and churches at Elveden, page 83; and Lakenheath, page 87.

Bruisyard
Bruisyard Wines, page 120.

Above: *The butter cross in Bungay is topped with a statue of Justice.*

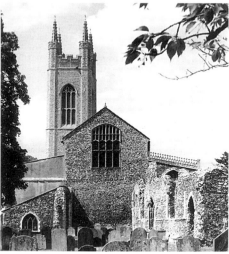

Left: *St Mary's church, Bungay, with the nunnery ruins on the right.*

Bungay

OS 156: TM 336897. Population 4710.
Market day Thursday.

In a defensive loop of the river Waveney, Bungay was a medieval stronghold of the Bigod family until around 1300, its Benedictine nunnery having been founded by Gundreda Bigod in 1160. Its greatest periods of prosperity occurred in the twelfth and eighteenth centuries, the latter arising from the 1670 act of Parliament granting navigation of the river, generating a series of locks and greatly stimulating trade. Just a few years later, the 1688 Great Fire badly damaged four hundred buildings and melted the church bells, but Bungay rebuilt itself as a spa with

Georgian streets of red-brick façades with Dutch gables and elaborate doorcases. The spa waters sprang from the Bath Hills, now in Norfolk. Since that time, Bungay has been best-known for printing and is the only English town still with a Town Reeve, effectively its chief magistrate.

The fire missed St Mary's church and tower, the four pinnacles of which dominate the town. Within the churchyard are the ruins of Gundreda's nunnery and the Druid's Stone, a glacial erratic; beyond is Holy Trinity church with its Saxon round tower of herringbone masonry.

The octagonal, domed Butter Cross in the centre was built in 1689 in commemoration of the fire; its lead statue of Justice was added in 1754. In Market Square is a lamp-post carrying a weathervane depicting the Black Dog of Bungay or 'Black Shuck' – presumably named after Thor's mythical dog Shukr – a wild hound which reputedly rampaged through a thunderstorm in the mid sixteenth century and killed two people. On the same night Blythburgh's church spire collapsed and the Devil left his scorch marks on the north door. Around Market Square the streets are historic, offering several routes to the castle; Castle Lane passes a romantic riverside turret built in 1839; Castle Orchard leads to Castle Hills, a public viewpoint over meadows and woodland.

Bungay Castle, page 73; **Bungay Museum**, page 102.

In the locality: Mettingham Castle, page 77; Norfolk and Suffolk Aviation Museum, page 104; the Otter Trust, page 122; St Cross Farm Walks, page 67; and church at Barsham with Shipmeadow, page 80.

Bures
Arger Fen, page 61.

Bury St Edmunds
OS 155: TL 853645. Population 33,440.
Market days Wednesday and Saturday.
Edmund was crowned king on Christmas Day AD 855 at Bures St Mary and became the focus of resistance to the occupying Danes. He led his army against them but was captured and executed in 869. Afterwards, the Danes hid Edmund's severed head, but leg-

end has it that the head called out and was found by Edmund's followers, having been guarded by a wolf. Some of these events are portrayed in medieval wall-paintings at St Mary, Thornham Parva, and in bench-end carvings at St Mary, Hadleigh. Within living memory of Edmund's death, memorial coins were struck and in 1020 Bury St Edmunds was renamed in his honour, becoming a national centre of pilgrimage.

A place of such significance was felt to warrant an abbey, so a huge edifice rose in the early twelfth century. Little survives beyond its Norman tower and the accompanying new town built to a gridiron plan by Abbot Baldwin. The abbey was completed, but growing monastic wealth attracted censure and in 1327 it was sacked in a public riot; the gateway was rebuilt twenty years later as a show of strength. At the Dissolution in 1539, Bury was one of the wealthiest towns in Eng-

Abbey Gate, Bury St Edmunds.

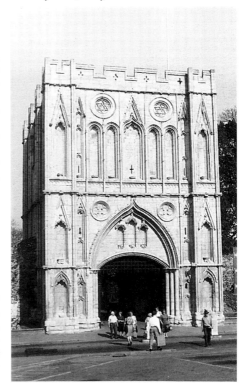

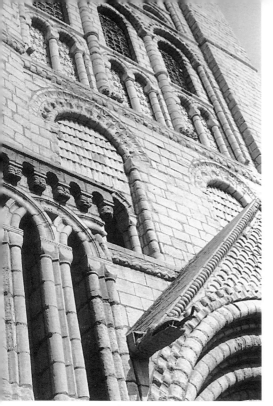

Above left: *The Norman tower of Bury St Edmunds Abbey.*
Above right: *Cupola House in Bury St Edmunds.*

land, its abbey one of the greatest in Europe.

A town fire in 1608 promoted some good new buildings; a century later the gentry were attracted by a spa, from which time much of the present Georgian character remains. Bury was little changed by the industrial revolution, remaining an agricultural centre, but there are fine mid nineteenth-century churches such as Grecian St Edmund and brick-spired St John. The 1846 arrival of the railway brought expansion and an impressive Corn Exchange in 1861. Bury is now a thriving and sophisticated market town.

Town walk

Start on Angel Hill, which from the middle ages to 1871 was the site of the annual Bury Fair, at that time extending to Chequer Square. On the upper side, the creeper-clad Angel Hotel has connections with Charles Dickens and is built over thirteenth-century vaults. Leave Angel Hill, passing between the front

of St Edmundsbury Cathedral and the stuccoed Athenaeum, built in 1714 to become the centre of Bury's social life. Continue past the Norman tower, beautifully carved and gargoyled, which leads from Churchgate Street to the remains of the abbey's west front, ruined, romantic and quarried. Houses have been built into it over the last three hundred years. Chequer Square is lined with Georgian buildings and includes a Georgian obelisk. Continue to Crown Street, passing Honey Hill and Sparhawk Street en route to the Saxon market place of St Mary's Square in the lee of the huge brick Greene King brewery. A slight detour past Westgate Street and the timber-framed buildings of Southgate Street leads past Norman Bridewell Lane and College Street, which are typical of the town.

Pass Whiting Street, once occupied by whitening makers, and St Edmund's church, to walk the full length of Guildhall Street with its miscellaneous pargeting, timber framing, rubbed brickwork and greatly modified guild-hall. This leads on to Cornhill with its generous Corn Exchange and the tiny Nutshell, probably Britain's smallest pub. Cupola House of 1693 retains a rooftop observatory. All around this Buttermarket area are fine buildings and on market days countless people and stalls.

Along Out Risbygate, by the Suffolk Regiment Museum, is the Old Plague Stone, a former St Peter's cross filled in times of plague with vinegar and used in an attempt to sterilise coins.

Bury Festival of the Arts is held each May.

Abbey, page 74; **Abbey Gardens**, page 97; **Abbey Visitor Centre**, page 102; **Bury St Edmunds Art Gallery**, page 102; **church of St Mary**, page 80; **Greene King Brewery**, page 116; **Manor House Museum**, page 102, **Moyse's Hall Museum**, page 103; **St Edmundsbury Cathedral**, page 80; **Suffolk Regiment Museum**, page 103; **Theatre Royal**, page 101; **Unitarian Meeting House**, page 82.

In the locality: Anglo-Saxon Village, page 71; Bardwell Windmill, page 114; Cow Wise, page 120; Hengrave Hall, page 98; Ickworth House, page 98; Lackford Wildfowl Reserve, page 65; Lark Valley Path, page 65; Netherfield Herb Garden, page 122; Pakenham Watermill, page 117; Rede Hall Farm Park, page 121; Stanton Windmill, page 118; West Stow Country Park, page 69; and churches at Hessett, page 86; Icklingham, page 86; Rushbrooke, page 91; and Stowlangtoft, page 94.

Butley

Butley Priory Gatehouse, page 75; Staverton Thicks, page 68; Suffolk Heritage Coast Path, path 68.

Carlton Colville

Carlton Marshes, page 62; East Anglia Transport Museum, page 106.

Cavendish

OS 155: TL 805465. Population 1000.

The village sign shows the killing of Wat Tyler, the peasants' champion, at Smithfield by Richard II's squire John Cavendish, whose manor occupied this village. In retribution, his father, Lord Chief Justice of England, was apparently chased by peasants and beheaded in the market place at Bury St Edmunds. Such events contrast with today's tranquillity in this upper reach of the river Stour.

The picturesque, gently sloping village green is surrounded by scattered colour-washed houses, a thatched pub, the old grammar school and the fourteenth-century church. The main street with its Gothick windows and grapevine pargeting leads gently away, curving past the duck pond and on, beside almshouses with huge chimneys, into a gently rolling arable landscape.

Cavendish Manor Vineyard, page 120; **Pentlow Farm**, page 121; **Sue Ryder Foundation Museum**, page 103.

In the locality: Clare Castle, page 75; Clare Country Park, page 62; Clare Priory, page 75; Kentwell Hall, page 99; Kentwell Hall Home Farm, page 121; Melford Hall, page 99; and church at Long Melford, page 90.

Cavenham

Cavenham Heath National Nature Reserve, page 62.

Charsfield

Akenfield, page 97.

Clare

OS 155: TL 770454. Population 1980.

Clare was a prehistoric camp at the strategic head of the river Stour – gateway to East Anglia from the North Sea. In 1066, as one of ten boroughs in Suffolk, Clare was ceded to the Bienfait family who helped draw up Magna Carta and probably built its first castle.

The town is small and attractive with many interesting buildings, especially in Nethergate Street, with Regency Clarence House, Nethergate House rebuilt in 1644 and The Cliftons with its ornate chimneys. There are good shopfronts and signs, like that of the Swan Hotel, built around 1440; carvings over the front door may have come from the castle. The best-known frontage belongs to the Ancient House, a priest's home in 1473; the remarkable pargeting was applied later. Nearby is the notable thirteenth-century church of St Peter and St Paul, linked to the great medieval family who founded Clare

Pargeting on the Ancient House, Clare.

College at Cambridge. A Georgian sundial enlivens the south porch.

Clare Castle, page 75; **Clare Country Park**, page 62; **Clare Priory**, page 75.

In the locality: Cavendish Manor Vineyard, page 120; Pentlow Farm, page 121; Sue Ryder Foundation Museum, page 103; church at Denston, page 82.

Cockfield
Bulls Wood, page 62.

Combs
Combs Wood, page 62.

Cotton
Mechanical Music Museum Trust, page 103.

Covehithe
Church of St Andrew, page 82.

Creeting St Peter
Fen Alder Carr, page 63.

Dalham
OS 154: TL 723616. Population 200.
Picturesque Dalham offers a main street of thatched and well-spaced houses running parallel with the young river Kennet. In one garden stands a small conical brickwork tower, an early malt kiln. Some distance up-hill, reached either through a double avenue of horse-chestnut trees or along a wooded lane, is the fourteenth-century church. Its spire fell, to be replaced with a tower in 1627 by a man who 'saw the new world with Francis Drake'. The south side proclaims 'Keep my Sabbaths' – for the benefit of the villagers, whose memorials include one to a 'punctual poultrywoman'. The church roof was restored in memory of Cecil Rhodes, who bought adjacent Dalham Hall, elevated in 1705 by the Bishop of Ely, who hoped to be able to see his cathedral on a fine day. Dalham's smock mill (no public access) stands on high ground across the valley.

In the locality is the picturesque village of **Lidgate** (OS 154: TL 725577), home to the poet John Lydgate, born in 1370, who wrote a famous *Life of St Edmund*.

Darsham
Darsham Marshes, page 63.

Debenham

OS 156: TM 174634. Population 1850.
Debenham's Blood Field perhaps recalls a battle with the Danes. In those days the town was an important centre and court of the East Anglian kings. In 1221 the market was chartered and a market-town character remains today; the only trace of the priory is Priory Field.

The town is situated in rich clay farmland along a harmonious undulating main street, generally broad but partly infilled with isolated buildings like the Market Cross, which in 1668 was converted to Sir Robert Hitcham's School. The varying width of this street is evidence of a fire in 1744 and a history of gradual change. There are several old pubs and many pretty cottages, a few of which have been greatly modified, forming large passageways into back courts, some overlooking the stream.

The ancient description of Debenham as 'High Church, Low Steeple, Drunken Parson, Wicked People' may have related to its prowess in cidermaking and perhaps recalled the direct hit by lightning in 1667 on the modified Saxon church tower.

In the locality: British Birds of Prey and Conservation Centre, page 122; Framsden Windmill, page 115; Helmingham Hall Gardens, page 98; James White's Apple Juice and Cider Company, page 120; Mickfield Fish and Water Garden Centre, page 122; Mid-Suffolk Light Railway Society Museum, page 109; Otley Hall, page 100.

Dennington

Church of St Mary the Virgin, page 82.

Denston

Church of St Nicholas, page 82.

Dunwich

OS 156: TM 475705. Population 130.
Dunwich was an episcopal see in AD 630 with a cathedral forty years later, but it suffered from the Danish invasion of 870. By Domesday it had recovered, as an annual tax of 68,000 herrings testifies. Under Henry II (reigned 1154-89) Dunwich expanded to become a port of national importance, sheltering five galleys and eighty ships, and having twelve churches, two monasteries, a mint and two hospitals within the town ramparts. Because it was built where the river Blyth then entered the sea, Dunwich controlled access to Blythburgh, Southwold and Walberswick and thereby trade with Scandinavia and France in grain, cloth, wool, salt, iron, furs, pitch and building stone. Not surprisingly, there was a market every single weekday. All this was halted by inundations in 1286 and 1328, when the shingle spit protecting the harbour was destroyed; trade then passed to Blythburgh.

Two parish churches were taken by the sea before 1300; fifty years later four hundred houses were washed away in a single night. In 1677 the waves reached the market place and in 1739 the town centre collapsed. In 1904 Swinburne described the condition of All Saints, which had gone by 1919:

'...one hollow tower and hoary
Naked in the sea wind stands and moans.
Filled and thrilled with its perpetual story;
Here where earth is dense with dead men's bones.'

Legend has it that on stormy nights church bells can be heard tolling below the waves.

Much of the present Victorian village is due to Frederick Barnes, who built commodious houses with pretty glazing bars and steep roofs under crested ridges.

Overlooking marshland, fishing huts and boats, a car park now marks the site of the Maison Dieu founded by Henry III (reigned 1216-72); it survived until about 1750. Nearby, a footpath leads along the very edge of Dunwich Cliff, into a grove of thorn trees sheltering the remains of All Saints' graveyard, then back through Greyfriars to the village, where St James's church was built in 1820 on the site of a medieval leper hospital; the apse of its Norman chapel survives nearby.

Dunwich Greyfriars, page 75; **Dunwich Heath and Common**, page 63; **Dunwich Museum**, page 104.

In the locality: Minsmere Nature Reserve, page 66; Suffolk Heritage Coast Path, page 68; Westleton Heath National Nature Reserve, page 69.

Above: *Bells in the churchyard ringing chamber at East Bergholt.*

Below: *Visitors enjoying the sunshine at Flatford Mill.*

East Bergholt

OS 155, 169: TM 075353. Population 2590.

East Bergholt prospered from the cloth trade until Regency times but is now best-known for views over Dedham Vale and for the artist John Constable (1776-1837), who recorded many of them. Much of the town has a Georgian character, but there is an ornate Victorian church, Italianate Old Hall and curios such as a 'Dealer in Hatts' sign. The large stone tower of St Mary's church was begun in 1525 but never completed, perhaps because of a downturn in the cloth industry or Wolsey's fall from power, and the five heavy bells are hand-rung from an unusual open-work timber-framed bell-house, built at ground level in 1530 in the churchyard, where members of the Constable family are buried.

A road from East Bergholt leads down to the Stour floodplain and the tiny settlement of **Flatford**, where the watermill, on the site of one worked by John Constable's father, is now a picturesque field centre. Constable's painting 'The Haywain' illustrates this scene, and 'Willy Lott's Cottage', a typical Suffolk yeoman's house built about 1600, still stands near the restored Flatford Lock.

In the locality: Bridge Cottage, page 97.

Easton

OS 156: TM 284588. Population 350.

Situated on the higher side of the river Deben,

The crinkle-crankle wall at Easton.

Easton is a pretty village which owes its rustic estate-village character to nineteenth-century ownership by the Earls of Rochford and Dukes of Hamilton. Their house is enclosed by a long winding crinkle-crankle wall, maybe the finest in Suffolk. Around the village is an attractive collection of buildings with Gothick windows and conical thatched roofs.

Easton Farm Park, page 120.

In the locality: Akenfield, page 97; Letheringham Watermill, page 116; Valley Farm Camargue Horses and White Animal Collection, page 123.

Ellough
Church of All Saints, page 82.

Elveden
Church of St Andrew and St Patrick, page 83.

Eriswell
OS 143: TL 725781. Population 4590.
Lying between the Fens and Breckland, Eriswell is an attractive thatched and flint-built village which for two hundred years was associated with the New England Company, whose NEC initials can be seen on a number of buildings. From 1649 money was raised to support the company's policy of sending missionaries abroad to convert the North American Indians. Occasionally an Indian came to Eriswell; one fourteen-year-old immigrant who arrived in 1818 survived only two years and his memorial is in St Laurence's churchyard.

In 1863 Eriswell was sold to Maharajah Duleep Singh and later to the Earl of Iveagh, both men of immense wealth. Each remodelled the astonishingly oriental Elveden Hall, which is closed to the public. A local curiosity is the Dove House at Eriswell Hall Farm; it is all that remains of old St Peter's church.

In the locality: Mildenhall and District Museum, page 107; RAF Lakenheath, page 123; churches at Elveden, page 83; Lakenheath, page 87; and Mildenhall, page 91.

Euston
Church of St Genevieve, page 83; Euston Hall, page 97.

Eye
OS 144, 156: TM 145738. Population 1770.
Early closing Tuesday.
Eye – Saxon for island – was protected by the river Dove, then by William Malet's castle, in the lee of which it grew quickly. Its new market was sufficiently successful to ruin the nearby village of Hoxne and Eye's expansion was assisted by its priory, which received

Eye town centre, showing its variety of old shopfronts, timber framing, decorative chimneys and classical refronting.

tithes from Dunwich. The town was elevated to a borough in 1408 but by 1970 it was the smallest one in England.

The Bedingfield Almshouses were built in 1636 to house four poor widows; modification in 1850 included the inscriptions 'Believe Right; Doe Well; Avoid Ill for Heaven'. They border a wide main street which rises to the island site of the domed and clock-towered town hall (1857), its patterned walls of red and white bricks with flint diamonds recalling Eye's success in lacemaking at that time. All around are winding and tapering roads with changing views to old shopfronts, refronted houses, memorials and curios like the arched entry to the 'Posting Establishment'. Jetted and colourwashed houses, densely packed together yet retaining intimacy, are reached up little flights of steps. Lanes like Hartshorn Street lead to the fine early sixteenth-century guildhall, where the Archangel Gabriel is carved on a corner post.

Eye Show is held each summer and the town supports a good local theatre.

Church of St Peter and St Paul, page 83;

Eye Castle, page 75.

In the locality: Mechanical Music Museum Trust, page 103; Mid-Suffolk Light Railway Society Museum, page 109; Thornham Walks, page 69; churches at Braiseworth, page 80; Wingfield, page 95; Wortham, page 95.

Farnham

George E. Cook, basketmaker, page 115.

Felixstowe

OS 169: TM 305345. Population 23,790.
Early closing Wednesday; market days Thursday and Sunday.

Abundant sunshine, dry summers and sandy beaches have attracted holidaymakers to Felixstowe for generations. The railway arrived in 1877, creating a fashionable resort with spa waters and gardens which entertained the Empress of Germany in 1891. A less enthusiastic resident during the 1936 abdication crisis was Mrs Wallis Simpson, who should have enjoyed the 2 mile (3 km) promenade from Cobbold's Point to the Manor House, with its half-mile (800 metre) pier, now truncated. Electric trams once ran its full length to meet steamers from Great Yarmouth and London; the steamers have been replaced by huge container ships bound for Zeebrugge.

Felixstowe is easily the largest container port in Britain and fourth in Europe. The dock opened in 1886 but was relatively quiet until 1967, when 180 yards (165 metres) of purpose-built container quay was opened – the first in England. Trade increased, necessitating the 1986 Trinity Container Terminal for roll-on/roll-off cargo, able to handle over a million containers in twelve months – a third of the whole United Kingdom container cargo. Current expansion allows the world's largest ships to be accommodated here on a quay nearly a mile and a half (2.4 km) long, unloaded by cranes reaching out over 60 yards (55 metres). There are public viewpoints, including Fagbury Point, accessible from Trimley.

Seafront Felixstowe has a good collection of opulent Edwardian buildings, especially atop the low cliff which looks down to extensive colourful Seafront Gardens and the Pier Bight with its fast food, bingo and leisure centre.

Further north, beyond lines of multi-coloured beach-huts overlooking The Dip, Old Felixstowe extends beyond a sandy sea-side golf course between two martello towers. The road ends at Felixstowe Ferry, a fishing hamlet with timbered shanties, good marine views and sometimes a passenger ferry across the shingly mouth of the river Deben to Bawdsey.

7 miles (11 km) offshore, built on the seabed, stands the wartime fort of Rough Tower. It is now privately owned, having claimed to be an independent principality.

Felixstowe launched early aerial attacks on submarines and zeppelins in the First World War and after the Armistice, 150 U-boats surrendered in the river Stour. From 1913 to 1963 Felixstowe was also the main seaplane test centre where the famous Schneider Trophy teams were formed in 1927-31. The many coastal gun emplacements and observation posts were assisted by radar, which was developed in the 1930s nearby at Bawdsey Manor by Robert Watson-Watt.

Church of St Andrew, page 83; **Felixstowe Museum**, page 104; **Landguard Fort**, page 76; **Landguard Point**, page 65.

Behind the sea wall at Felixstowe Ferry, a row of beach huts leads to the martello tower.

In the locality: Suffolk Heritage Coast Path, page 68; Trimley Marshes, page 69.

Flatford
See East Bergholt, page 20.

Flixton
Norfolk and Suffolk Aviation Museum, page 104.

Framlingham
OS 156: TM 285634. Population 2760. Early closing Wednesday; market day Saturday.

The heart of the town is Market Hill, a steep triangle of gentle commerce with pollarded limes fronting Mansion House, which is faced in mathematical tiles. Opposite, the Crown Hotel is a refronted former coaching inn; it extends over Queen's Head Alley, from whence a pleasant stroll leads to Fairfield Meadow. Lower down Market Hill the 1717 Unitarian chapel retains doors segregating the sexes. A walk around the town should not miss Double Street, an attractive quadrant of colourwashed and white brick houses. Other sights include a former flour mill converted into a church in 1867 and Jeaffreson's Well, sunk in 1896, now sheltered within a pavilion.

Seven-gabled Hitcham Almshouses were built in 1654. Further handsome almshouses followed in 1709, built from downtakings of Framlingham Castle by a local nonconformist preacher, Thomas Mills (1640-1703), after whom the local school is named. He was buried in front of his own house in Station Road in 1703 with his 'faithful servant William Mayhew'; about 1820 their Tudor-style mausoleum was erected on the same spot.

Church of St Michael the Archangel, page 83; **Framlingham Castle**, page 76; **Framlingham Mere**, page 64; **Lanman Museum**, page 105; **Shawsgate Vineyard**, page 121.

In the locality: 390th Bomb Group Memorial Air Museum, page 108; Bruisyard Wines, page 120; Easton Farm Park, page 120; Laxfield and District Museum, page 106; Letheringham Watermill, page 116; Martin's Meadow, page 66; Saxtead Green Post Mill, page 117; and church at Dennington, page 82.

Framsden
Framsden Windmill, page 115.

Fressingfield
Church of St Peter and St Paul, page 83.

Freston
Freston Woods, page 64.

Gipping
Church of St Nicholas, page 83.

Great Cornard
Cornard Mere, page 63.

Great Finborough
Church of St Andrew, page 83.

Groton
Groton Wood, page 64.

Hadleigh
OS 155: TM 025425. Population 6750. Early closing Wednesday; market days Friday and Saturday.

Hadleigh was for centuries under direct rule from Canterbury – hence the Deanery with its magnificent tower, built in 1495 as the three-storey gatehouse to a palace for Archdeacon Pykenham. Above an arched entrance, ornamental brickwork rises into polygonal turrets overlooking the Dean's study, where the Oxford Movement began in 1833. This is one of an exceptional group of medieval buildings around the large flint church which carries a dramatically leaded wooden spire, pinpointing Hadleigh's low site in the valley of the river Brett, where once stood the palace of King Guthrum (died AD 890), first Danish king of East Anglia. One viewpoint over the town is Aldham Common, where a memorial commemorates Hadleigh's rector, Dr Rowland Tayler, who was burnt at the stake during Queen Mary's persecutions of 1555.

Beside the Guildhall is the porticoed Corn Exchange, just off the tiny Market Place beside the High Street, where many old timber-framed buildings were later refronted – big-beamed interiors are visible through Victorian shopfronts. There are the lovely windows

Beyond the Market Place in Hadleigh is the porticoed Corn Exchange and, to the left, the Victorian extension to the Guildhall.

(dated 1676) and fine cornice of the old Coffee Tavern at numbers 62-6 High Street, just along from number 48, which displays a clock, pargeted vines and the arms of the Cavendish and Bayning families.

Angel Street, Benton Street and George Street are full of old houses hugging the narrow roads, their jetted and colourwashed fronts rubbing shoulders with almshouses and Victorian infill. Parts of Queen Street have Georgian fronts, whilst Duke Street leads to the medieval three-arched red-brick Toppesfield Bridge, beyond which are walks over Bullocky Fen.

Hadleigh Guildhall, page 97.

In the locality: Corn Craft, page 122; Groton Wood, page 64; Hintlesham Hall, page 98; Lindsey St James's Chapel, page 77; Wattisham Airfield Historical Collection, page 109; Wolves Wood, page 69; and church at Boxford, page 80.

Halesworth

OS 156: TM 385774. Population 5160.
Navigation of the river Blyth in 1756 greatly increased the trade of Halesworth's maltsters and brewers, improving communications with an outside world which looked so enticing that two generations of one brewing family, William and Joseph Hooker, left to become avid international plant collectors, explorers, botanists and eventually directors of Kew Gardens.

The Thoroughfare is the pleasantly colourwashed main shopping street, which has been much rebuilt, with even some Edwardian terracotta, yet retaining such features as a carved bressumer beam to number 6. A circular walk leaves the Thoroughfare at Bridge Street, crossing the stream by a footbridge and following the crinkle-crankle wall to Chediston Street and up into Market Place, dwarfed by some large old buildings. From here, a path through the churchyard past the almshouses reveals Gothic House, home of the Bedingfield family from 1540, with its jetted first floor, hooded windows and strange Jacobean porch.

Halesworth and District Museum, page 105.

In the locality: Holton Windmill, page 116; Toby's Walks, page 69; and churches at Blythburgh, page 80; Bramfield, page 80; Huntingfield, page 86; and Wenhaston, page 94.

Hartest
Gifford's Hall Vineyard, page 120.

Haughley
Haughley Park, page 98.

Haverhill
OS 154: TL 672455. Population 19,600.
Haverhill lay on the Roman road from Colchester to Cambridge and its market began in 1222 on Peas Market Hill, a site now wedged between the churchyard and Chediston Place, which was burnt in 1665. Much was rebuilt in Victorian red and yellow brick terraces for the thousands working in the town's rope and horsehair factories. That manufacture was founded on earlier skills, brought together in Gurteen's textile works (1784), the profits from which funded the opulent town hall, built in 1883 and restored in 1994 as the town's arts centre.

In 1955 Haverhill became one of the London's expanding towns, with proposals to grow from 4000 to 30,000 – an attempt to save an industrial town from dying. Limited expansion has generated a number of 1960s housing estates and industrial buildings around the centre. Amongst them are points of interest, such as the prominently spired red-brick United Reformed church and, nearby, Anne of Cleves House, reputedly built in 1540 by Henry VIII as his marriage settlement to her, and restored in 1986.

In the locality: Boyton Vineyard, page 120; Ladygate Wood, page 65; and churches at Denston, page 82; and Kedington, page 87.

Helmingham
Helmingham Hall Gardens, page 98.

Hengrave
Hengrave Hall, page 98.

Herringfleet
Church of St Margaret, page 86; Herringfleet Windpump, page 116.

Hessett
Church of St Ethelbert, page 86.

Hintlesham
Hintlesham Hall, page 98.

Hollesley
Hollesley Heath, page 64; Simpson's Saltings, page 67.

Holton
Holton Windmill, page 116.

Hopton
Hopton Fen, page 64.

Horringer
Ickworth House, page 98.

Huntingfield
Church of St Mary, page 86.

Icklingham
Church of All Saints, page 86.

Iken
Iken Cliff, page 65.

Ilketshall St Andrew
See the Saints Country, page 42.

Ipswich
OS 169: TM 165445. Population 119,000.
Market days Tuesday, Friday and Saturday.
Ipswich is the county town and a port at the head of the Orwell estuary, 12 miles (19 km) from the sea. Originally *Gipes Wic* (the dwelling place of the Saxon Gipi), it was thriving by the seventh century, trading across the North Sea in textiles, fish and metalwork, probably enjoying special patronage from Raedwald's palace at Rendlesham. It was also a Saxon centre for pottery, producing 'greyware' pots and pitchers. The Saxon market place occupied today's Cornhill, from where the market cross was plucked in 1812, and where the distinguished red and white Lloyds Bank of 1889 was opened out in 1929 to create Lloyds Avenue.

The town plan was consolidated by AD 991-1010, when defensive ditches were dug, including Tower Ramparts, which survives in name only. In 1200, well represented by the religious orders, Ipswich was chartered by

King John and so flourished that by 1520 it was England's sixth or seventh richest town.

Wolsey's Gate in College Street was built at this time, a surviving part of the Cardinal College of St Mary, begun in 1527 but demolished when its patron, Thomas Wolsey (page 125), fell from power, unable to support Henry VIII's wish to marry Anne Boleyn. Christchurch Mansion was built a few years later, from 1548, contemporary with a host of impressive timber-framed buildings including seafarers' and merchants' houses, especially around Fore Street, an interesting neighbourhood of docks, medieval churches and the Jewish cemetery by St Clement. At the junction with Grimwade Street there once stood a house owned by Thomas Cavendish (1555-92), the second Englishman to circumnavigate the globe, who reduced Acapulco to ashes, pirated a 700 ton ship off California and came home via the East Indies. Further along Grimwade Street, buildings from the 1630s include The Captains' Houses at numbers 79-83; then along Fore Street itself old warehouses include the workshops of the Tudor merchant Isaac Lord. Nearer the site of Wolsey's college, St Peter's Street and Silent Street contain many timber-framed buildings

from the fifteenth century. Another fine building from that time is the former Royal Oak inn at number 7 Oak Lane, off Northgate Street.

The Sparrowe family prospered through the seventeenth century, buying the Ancient House in Buttermarket in 1603 and applying to it in 1670 'Ipswich' windows, the arms of Charles II and a remarkable display of pargeting illustrating the continents of Europe (depicted by a Gothic church), America (a tobacco pipe), Asia (a domed structure) and Africa (a crocodile). Australia was not yet discovered. Only a generation later, the optimism of the Glorious Revolution encouraged a spectacular redecoration of St Margaret's nave roof and the construction of the wonderful Unitarian meeting house (page 87).

This promising start to the eighteenth century was not sustained, for the population of Ipswich dropped in Georgian times; yet there are a few Georgian houses of note, some in Lower Brook Street. The town's economic recovery came after the Napoleonic Wars through stimulation of the corn and malt trade and rapid growth in agricultural engineering.

From 1839 to 1842 Ipswich Wet Dock was

Christchurch Mansion in Ipswich is popular with school parties. The seventeenth-century building is now a museum.

constructed, cutting off a section of the river Gipping by excavating New Cut. The dock was a major undertaking, stretching over 26 acres (11 hectares), the largest of its type in England. In 1845 it gained an exceptional customs house built over a bonded warehouse. All around, visible from Ipswich Historic Waterfront Trail, huge industrial buildings remain, some already converted like the fine Contship Building which was once a malting warehouse.

The arrival of the railway brought new opportunities and the population of Ipswich increased dramatically in the 1840s. There was much new building in Italianate style, most notably in the large villas bordering Christchurch Park along Fonnereau Road and in business areas like Museum Street. Growing Victorian civic pride produced in 1867 the Town Hall with its statues of Commerce, Agriculture, Learning and Justice, followed in 1880 by the Post Office with its statues of Commerce, Industry, Electricity and Steam. The same Victorian spirit raised elaborate church towers and spires decorated in flushwork like those of St Mary-le-Tower (1870) and St Lawrence (1882).

Ipswich underwent considerable development in the 1960s. This brought such innovations as a spiral underground car park hidden next to the excellent Wolsey Theatre. From there, Civic Drive leads down to the pioneering, award-winning, piano-shaped dark glass Willis Faber office building. Finished in 1975, it is reflective by day, translucent by night, and its box-hedged roof garden can be glimpsed from the street.

Although the modern town has no cathedral or abbey, Ipswich has in recent years become more aware of the national importance of its Saxon origins and medieval heritage. The castle, town walls and gates have long been taken down (Westgate and Northgate surviving until the late eighteenth century). Of the two Augustinian priories, Trinity was replaced by Christchurch Mansion; the other was dissolved, leaving only a gateway and church. Yet the recent Buttermarket shopping development has brought new use to the redundant St Stephen's church as a tourist information centre from which town walks are organised.

Ipswich artists include John Moore (1821-1902), master of boisterous seascapes, and the watercolourist Leonard Squirrel (1893-1979),

Italianate villas in Fonnereau Road, Ipswich.

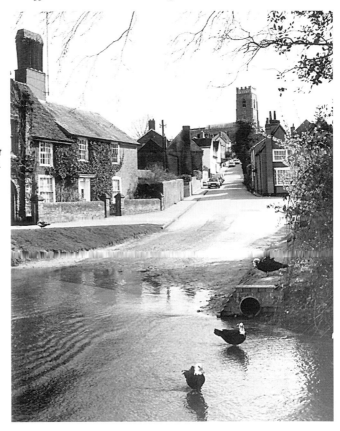

The ford and church at Kersey.

who painted urban panoramas; those of Ipswich are precise records crowded with detail.

Christchurch Mansion and Wolsey Art Gallery, page 105; **church of St Margaret**, page 87; **Ipswich Museum and Exhibition Gallery**, page 105; **Ipswich Transport Museum**, page 106; **Pykenham's Gatehouse**, page 100; **Tolly Cobbold Brewery and the Brewery Tap**, page 118; **Unitarian Meeting House**, page 87.

In the locality: Blakenham Woodland Garden, page 97; Freston Woods, page 64; Gipping Valley River Path, page 64; Hintlesham Hall, page 98; James White's Apple Juice and Cider Company, page 120; Nacton Meadows, page 66.

Kedington
Church of St Peter and St Paul, page 87.

Kersey
OS 155: TM 000442. Population 340.
Kersey is a picturesque settlement in the Brett valley. Once a cloth town, it is now a village whose main street falls steeply to a ford much loved by ducks, then rises sharply to the church. There are atmospheric weavers' cottages, merchants' houses and old pubs, big tapering chimneys, ancient brickwork, substantial timber frames and fine windows – as at Hedge End. Surrounding farmland can be glimpsed in breaks between mossy-tiled roofs and over the walls of well-stocked gardens.

In the locality: Groton Wood, page 64; Lindsey St James's Chapel, page 77.

Kessingland
Suffolk Wildlife Park, page 123.

Knettishall

Knettishall Heath Country Park, page 65.

Lackford

Lackford Wildfowl Reserve, page 65.

Lakenheath

Church of St Mary, page 87; Lakenheath Poors Fen, page 65; RAF Lakenheath, page 123.

Lavenham

OS 155: TL 915494. Population 1720.
Lavenham's fortunes depended on the cloth industry, which by 1524 had propelled it to become the fourteenth richest town in England, possessing four guildhalls. When that industry declined, Lavenham declined also, just surviving through agriculture, yarn spinning and horsehair weaving, but not greatly changing. Now it is a photogenic centre of tourism, its timber-framed buildings having distorted crazily over the years.

Much evidence of the cloth industry remains; the wealthy clothiers' houses are closely studded and jetted, with oriel windows, big front doors and openings at first-floor level where hoists would have loaded wool, yarn and cloth. Water Street, so called because it apparently runs above a stream once used for dyeing and fulling, includes many old houses.

The centre of the town is Market Place with its market cross from 1501; the shaft is much later. Here is a fine collection of buildings, such as Little Hall and the Guildhall of Corpus Christi. In Lady Street the Old Wool Hall was Our Lady's Guildhall in 1464. In 1911 it was dismantled and carried to Ascot but an outcry forced its return, to become part of the Swan Hotel in 1963. Mercers' Hall, however, was taken to Walberswick by traction engine in the 1920s, and there it remains. Church Street is studded with lovely old houses such as Blaize House and numbers 85-90. Barn Street includes Molet House, a fine clothier's house, and the Old Grammar School, where John Constable studied.

Church of St Peter and St Paul, page 87; **Guildhall of Corpus Christi**, page 106; **Little Hall**, page 99; **The Priory**, page 100.

In the locality: Bulls Wood, page 62; Corn Craft, page 122; Kentwell Hall, page 99; Kentwell Hall Home Farm, page 121; Melford Hall, page 99; church at Long Melford, page 90.

Laxfield

OS 156: TM 294723. Population 890.
Laxfield lies along a main street from which a network of pathways fans out around the village, past old brick walls and on to remoter farmhouses, the 'Tank Pond' of the Mid-Suffolk Railway and the infant river Blyth. At the centre is an irregular collection of old pargeted houses and gardens.

On the walls of the old Baptist chapel a plaque records the burning at the stake of John Noyes on 22nd September 1557. By then the pretty guildhall built for the Guild of St Mary in 1515 would already have been redundant. Its jetted oak frame and diagonal brick nogging now house a museum. Across the road is Laxfield's substantial church, with a fine barrel-vaulted roof spanning 35 feet (11 metres), an unusual font and eighteenth-century box pews.

East of England Birds of Prey and Conservation Centre, page 122; **Laxfield and District Museum**, page 106.

Leiston

OS 156: TM 445625. Population 5690.
Early closing Wednesday.
Industrial Leiston grew through the nineteenth century with the success of the Garrett family, who constructed their first threshing machine in 1806. Later they demonstrated a portable steam engine at London's Great Exhibition in 1851 and hundreds were ordered, requiring a new factory and a workforce of three hundred. Thus the Long Shop was built, one of the earliest production-line assembly halls in existence. The output was considerable, ranging from self-moving engines to traction engines and steam rollers. By the early 1900s the workforce topped one thousand, and the new Station Works was built. There followed fabrication of all kinds: steam wagons, Fe2b aircraft, heavy guns and even trolley buses. Falling orders resulted in closure in the 1960s, hitting Leiston badly, but alternative employment came from the nearby nuclear power stations.

Lavenham's church of St Peter and St Paul.

Church of St Mary of Antioch, page 90;
Leiston Abbey, page 77; **The Long Shop
Museum**, page 106.

*In the locality: Hazelwood Marshes, page
64; Minsmere Nature Reserve, page 66;
Moot Hall Museum, page 102; North Warren, page 67; Sizewell Visitor Centre, page
118.*

Letheringham
Letheringham Watermill, page 116.

Lidgate
See Dalham, page 18.

Lindsey
Lindsey St James's Chapel, page 77.

Little Blakenham
Blakenham Woodland Garden, page 97.

Long Melford
OS 155: TL 864455. Population 3320.
Long Melford's position at the confluence of
five Roman roads helped it become an impor-
tant settlement on the river Stour. Later, the
Abbots of Bury kept a hunting lodge here.

The town flourished from the manufacture of
cloth, diversifying into mat making, horsehair weaving and ironfounding. It was also a
staging post on the coaching road to London.

The town really is long, its wide main
street extending some 3 miles (5 km). The
road descends across a huge, impressive 14
acre (6 hectare) triangular green, once the
site of market fairs and medieval processions.
The small brick building standing there now
is a conduit house erected around 1550 above
a wooden-piped water supply. All around the
green are fine houses from the fifteenth to
eighteenth centuries, some with impressive
gateways. Larger buildings include the Hospital of the Holy and Undivided Trinity, completed in 1573 as almshouses for twelve men
and two servants, but reconstructed from the
basement up in 1847. The green tapers towards
the Chad Brook bridge.

Beyond the bridge is a broad generous
street full of antique shops and chapels, galleries, boutiques and pubs, of which the best
known is the Bull.

Church of the Holy Trinity, page 90;
Kentwell Hall, page 99; **Kentwell Hall
Home Farm**, page 121.

In the locality: Cavendish Manor Vineyard, page 120; Gifford's Hall Vineyard, page 120; Guildhall of Corpus Christi, page 106; Little Hall, page 99; Melford Hall, page 99; Pentlow Farm, page 121; The Priory, page 100; Sue Ryder Foundation Museum, page 103; and churches at Lavenham, page 87; and Sudbury, page 94.

Lound
Church of St John, page 90.

Lowestoft
OS 134: TM 550925. Population 58,200.
By the 1350s Lowestoft was well established as a fishing centre, becoming wealthy enough by 1480 to build the fine St Margaret's church. As early as 1609 the town had a lighthouse and from 1757 to 1799 its trade thrived on Lowestoft porcelain.

In 1820 Lake Lothing was dredged in an attempt to expand trade from Norwich; locks were built and cuts driven, but the port silted up, to be rescued, with the town, in the 1840s by Sir Morton Peto. In five years he built the fish market, wharves and warehouses as well as the Outer Harbour leading to the Inner Harbour and on to Oulton Broad. Fish curing and maritime industry flourished, expanding with the arrival of the railway in 1847. That led to the development of the South Town as a fashionable resort with hotels, smart terraces and two piers; the North Town answered back in 1857 with an Italianate town hall, refronted in 1899 during street widening. Wartime bomb damage in the town necessitated extensive rebuilding and the consequential mix of new and old buildings is at times disconcerting. Today, Lowestoft is more associated with oil, gas and frozen food than fishing.

From the Naval Memorial the clifftop road leads south above The Denes, where port industry, caravans and net-drying greens shelter behind the sea wall. The verdant Sparrow's Nest Gardens are named after Robert Sparrow, who founded a lifeboat society in 1800. Adjacent is the lighthouse of 1874 and steep Lighthouse Score, one of many narrow alleys leading down to the sea and which once contained smokehouses for herrings.

The gently curving High Street is full of old inns, antique shops and merchants' houses from the sixteenth century; there are also curios like the Armada Post, an historic block of wood recalling Lowestoft's provision of a fireship for the battle off Calais; it was last renewed on the four hundredth anniversary in 1988. Rant Score was the scene of a 1643 confrontation between Cromwellians and local Royalists.

A swing bridge joins the North to the South Town where the East Point Pavilion, an ogee-roofed glasshouse, is a tourist information centre. Adjacent, overlooking the harbour, is the lovely early twentieth-century Yacht Club with its round windows and copper dome. Here is the South Pier (reopened 1993), from where a sandy beach extends to Claremont Pier. Above runs the Esplanade, along which unfurl the Victorian terraces of Marine Parade (restrained, but with huge chimneys), Wellington Esplanade (getting grander) and, as the cliff gently rises again, Kirkley Cliff (heavily balconied).

Oulton Broad is the southern gateway to the Norfolk Broads, providing river cruising and power-boat racing.

East Anglia Transport Museum, page 106; **Fish Market and Harbour area**, page 116; **Foxburrow Wood**, page 63; **Leathes Ham**, page 66; **Lowestoft and East Suffolk Maritime Museum**, page 106; **Lowestoft Museum**, page 106; **Lydia Eva and Mincarlo**, page 116; **Royal Naval Patrol Service Association Museum**, page 106.

In the locality: Benacre National Nature Reserve, page 61; Boat World, page 114; Camps Heath and Oulton Marshes, page 62; Carlton Marshes, page 62; Herringfleet Windpump, page 116; Pleasurewood Hills American Theme Park, page 123; Somerleyton Hall, page 100; Suffolk Heritage Coast Path, page 68; Suffolk Wildlife Park, page 123; and churches at Covehithe, page 82; Herringfleet, page 86; and Lound, page 90.

Market Weston
Market Weston Fen, page 66.

Mellis
OS 144: TM 100745. Population 340.
The land here is as flat as a prairie, and one

Timber framing on Lavenham Little Hall.

part of it is Mellis. The centre of this village is a huge treeless green, impressively unenclosed, called The Carnser. It is contained by a thin line of houses, a towerless church and some powerful industrial buildings by the railway which strides through this unusual landscape. During the Second World War the green temporarily grew potatoes and grain; now it again extends 1400 acres (567 hectares). The church tower fell in 1735.

In the locality: Thornham Walks, page 69; Wortham Ling, page 69; and churches at Braiseworth, page 80; and Wortham, page 95.

Metfield
Winks Meadow, page 69.

Mettingham
Mettingham Castle, page 77.

Mickfield
Mickfield Fish and Water Garden Centre, page 122; Mickfield Meadow, page 66.

Mildenhall
OS 143: TL 712753. Population 13,490.
In north-west Suffolk, Mildenhall borders the Bedford Level, overlooking wide fenland which has been partly drained but retains a wild eerie beauty. Around 1042 the town and its rich pastureland were acquired by St Edmundsbury Abbey, which was linked to Mildenhall by the river Lark.

The town, damaged by fire in 1567, has in recent decades been modernised and expanded – it is close to a military base. Historic remains include the heavily timbered hexagonal market cross with its generous lead roof, still retaining a 1681 crest, and the nearby church between the priory and almshouses dated 1722. Past Mabbs Hall, amongst Victorian buildings more reminiscent of Cambridgeshire than Suffolk, Mill Street leads to some large brick mill buildings on the riverside.

Church of St Mary, page 91; **Mildenhall and District Museum**, page 107.
In the locality: Cavenham Heath National

Jetted timber-framed houses and the church at Stoke-by-Nayland.

Nature Reserve, page 62; Lark Valley Path, page 65; RAF Lakenheath, page 123; and churches at Elveden, page 83; Icklingham, page 86; and Lakenheath, page 87.

Monewden
Martin's Meadow, page 66.

Monks Eleigh
Corn Craft, page 122.

Moulton
OS 154: TL 696644. Population 1020.
In the lee of Primrose Hill is a collection of thatched colourwashed houses with flint walls and ornamental Victorian brickwork. Together with the manor and St Peter's church, these encircle a large village green, to one side of which runs the small river Kennet, providing some fords and two impressive old bridges of the packhorse type, arched in flint in the early fifteenth century.

Tradition has it that the roadside Gypsy Grave at OS 154: TL 687661 recalls a young shepherd who hanged himself in despair when one of his flock went missing.

Nacton

Nacton Meadows, page 66.

Nayland

OS 155: TL 975344.

Nayland's attractive narrow streets wind past the peaceful backwaters of the river Stour. Court Knoll, a moated field, was the town's Norman centre, of which nothing survives. Fourteenth-century St James's church, with its copper spire installed in 1963, displays an altar painting by John Constable. From its flamboyant porch, rebuilt in 1884, it is no distance to Alston Court, a fine timber jetted house with an intricately carved window and semicircular door-hood. An obelisk mile-stone leads on past the old Guildhall to Fen Street, where individual bridges lead house-holders over the brick-revetted millstream to their front doors. Amongst the Gothick deco-rations and plasterwork of Bear Street, a small gap between the houses gives access to Nayland Horse Watering.

Nearby **Stoke-by-Nayland** sits atop a ridge between the Stour and Box valleys, its four-pinnacled church tower a local land-mark. Beside the church are some excellent old houses, and the Guildhall and Maltings are notable in School Street.

In the locality: Arger Fen, page 61.

Needham Market

OS 155: TM 085550. Population 4350.
Early closing Tuesday.

Like nearby Stowmarket, location on the river Gipping along one of Suffolk's major roads made Needham Market a bustling small town. Its market was chartered in 1226. Growth was encouraged by the Bishop of Ely and old buildings in the High Street – such as numbers 3-4, built as a school in 1632 with materials from the old Guildhall – show that it prospered until an outbreak of plague around 1675. To try to contain that, chains were placed across the road at Chain Bridge and Chain House Farm. The town recovered, acquiring in 1744 one of the ear-liest private banks through the Alexander

Hawks Mill at Needham Market.

The front at Aldeburgh after snow.

Baskets for sale at Orford Crafts.

Eye church and guildhall from the castle mound.

family, who were prominent Quakers. A big boost to trade was the opening of the Ipswich to Stowmarket Navigation in 1793, along which fifteen locks in a distance of 17 miles (27 km) raised barges by 90 feet (27 metres). One lock is beside black-timbered Bosmere Mill; just downstream is sturdy brick Hawks Mill. Recreational Needham Lake has nothing to do with either of them; it occupies a gravel pit dug in the 1970s to build the A14. The town was home to the Reverend Uvedale, a botanist who reputedly introduced the cedar of Lebanon to Britain.

Church of St John the Baptist, page 91.

In the locality: Baylham House Rare Breeds Farm, page 120; Blakenham Woodland Garden, page 97; Bonny Wood, page 61; British Birds of Prey and Conservation Centre, page 122; Fen Alder Carr, page 63; Gipping Valley River Path, page 64; Wattisham Airfield Historical Collection, page 109.

Newbourne

OS 169: TM 275425. Population 280.

East of Ipswich, tiny Newbourne was a centre of the coprolite industry which flourished on the Felixstowe peninsula in the mid nineteenth century. Extraction began around 1718 when this fossilised material (dinosaur droppings) was first used as an artifical fertiliser at Levington. It was mined, dredged or dug, then washed and taken by barge to factories like Packard's Mill at Snape, where it was reacted with sulphuric acid to produce superphosphate of lime. The trade boomed between 1840 and 1880, profits being used, for example, to build the Mary Warner Homes at Boyton. Then, increasingly, this early chemical fertiliser industry declined, suffering from cheap surface-mined phosphates imported from America. Coprolite nodules, resembling fat stone sausages, can be found on some local beaches, and a local chemical fertiliser industry remains. Fisons was founded on this.

Newbourne was chosen by the government in the 1930s as the site for a land settlement project to help re-establish unemployed miners in agriculture. Many idealistic families, including Jarrow marchers, travelled from Durham to Newbourne's smallholdings in expectation of a new start in life, their produce being sold through a central administration. In 1983 the assets were sold off, but many of the chalet-style houses remain.

This scheme recalls the village of **Assington**, near Sudbury, which was organised co-operatively in accordance with the socialist theories of Robert Owen and was self-sufficient from 1845 to 1918, having its own currency of metal tokens.

Newbourne Springs, page 66.

Newmarket

OS 154: TL 645635. Population 16,840.
Early closing Tuesday; market days
Thursday and Saturday.

On the map, Newmarket occupies a little island of Suffolk in Cambridgeshire. It is dominated by horse-racing; over 2500 horses train here amidst some of Britain's most important studs and paddocks. Outside the town are mansions of the bloodstock industry; gaps in the dense roadside hedges reveal ostentatious gateways to enormous stable blocks crowned with clock-towers and cupolas.

Most mornings, strings of thoroughbreds travel from stable to training gallop along horse routes through the town. Small flint cottages and yellow brick terraces contrast with the big Victorian dwellings of racehorse owners and abundant, less attractive development covers wartime bombing scars. A broad, commercial High Street includes the Jockey Club; it runs from the Victorian Jubilee Clock-tower, stranded on a roundabout, to the 1910 neo-classical Sir Daniel Cooper Memorial Fountain overlooking the famous Heath. That lies to the west in Cambridgeshire, as do the racecourses.

King James I hunted here, coursing hares from 1605 and racing horses. Under Cromwell the sport was banned, to return at the Restoration with Charles II, whose court came to race each spring and summer. Charles instituted the Town Plate Race, which he won twice; some rooms from his 1670 palace remain at Palace House Mansion. The cottage of his mistress, Nell Gwyn, is also said to have survived Newmarket's fire of 1683 but it is not open to the public.

Church of St Agnes, page 91; **National Horseracing Museum**, page 107; **National**

Early morning training for racehorses at Newmarket.

Stud, page 122; **Palace House Mansion and Stables**, page 107.

North Cove
North Cove, page 66.

Onehouse
Northfield Wood, page 66.

Orford
OS 169: TM 423498. Population 690. Early closing Wednesday.

In the twelfth century Orford prospered from its royal castle and as a port on the river Ore, for at that time the spit now separating the river from the sea had not been formed. Until the 1550s there was trade with the Low Countries in fish and wool – hence the number of Dutch gables; then the harbour silted up. The writer Daniel Defoe recorded the decline in 1722: 'Orford was once a good town, but it decayed, the sea daily throws up more land to it, and falls off itself from it, as if it was resolved to disown the place, and that it should be a seaport no longer.'

Today it is a pleasant quiet village approached through coniferous forest, memorable for its two smokeries, its oysters cultivated in Butley Creek, for sailing from the quay and bracing walks across flood-protected marshes. Former town lanes have shrunk to paths amongst allotments in the lee of the castle's earthworks, and of the two medieval hospitals there is no trace.

Church of St Bartholomew, page 91; **Dunwich Underwater Exploration Exhibition**, page 108; **Orford Castle**, page 77.

In the locality: Butley Priory Gatehouse, page 75; Havergate Island National Nature Reserve, page 64; Orford Ness, page 122; Orford Ness National Nature Reserve, page 67; Staverton Thicks, page 68.

Otley
Otley College of Agriculture and Horticulture, page 121; Otley Hall, page 100.

Oulton Broad
Boat World, page 114; Camps Heath and Oulton Marshes, page 62; Lowestoft Museum, page 106.

Pakenham
Pakenham Watermill, page 117.

Parham
390th Bomb Group Memorial Air Museum, page 108.

Peasenhall
OS 156: TM 355694. Population 560.
Though separate parishes since the Norman

Left: *The House in the Clouds, Thorpeness.*

Below: *The annual regatta on Thorpeness Mere.*

A typical Suffolk building, with dormers, colourwash and pegtiles.

Thatched and colourwashed cottages at Ufford.

conquest, Peasenhall and its neighbour **Sibton** (OS 156: TM 360695) are effectively now one village, a long open settlement on the Roman road from Badingham, descending from the High Suffolk plateau. Sibton's abbey, the only Cistercian house in Suffolk, was founded in 1150, but its ruins now lie on private land. Peasenhall was best known for its drill works, built in 1800 just beside the churchyard, from whence agricultural drills were exported all over the world; the workers' reading room remains as a Swiss chalet-style village hall.

In the locality: Bruisyard Wines, page 120; East of England Birds of Prey and Conservation Centre, page 122.

Polstead
OS 155: TL 994383. Population 820.

This small village, named as a 'place of pools', occupies the northern slope of the Box valley round a large central pond in which witches were once 'swum'. The steep main street, peaceful cottage gardens and a one-time reputation for cherries contrast with the melodramatic murder of Maria Marten in 1837 at the Red Barn, which was burned down many years ago. The unusual brick arches inside the church may have been built by the Normans.

Rede
Rede Hall Farm Park, page 121.

Redgrave
Redgrave and Lopham Fens National Nature Reserve, page 67.

Rendlesham
Rendlesham Forest, page 67.

Reydon
Reydon Wood, page 67.

Rougham
Netherfield Herb Garden, page 122.

Rushbrooke
Church of St Nicholas, page 91.

St Cross South Elmham
St Cross Farm Walks, page 67.

St Margaret South Elmham
See the Saints Country (below).

The Saints Country
Around OS 156: TM 350854.

The Saints Country is a signally remote and rural area of Suffolk lying between Bungay and Halesworth. Tiny roads pass through its agricultural landscape whose regular fields perhaps date back to Roman times; the many hamlets are named after saints and are in two groups. The four Ilketshalls may refer to Alderman Alfketill, who routed the Danes in 1004; **Ilketshall St Andrew** includes seven commons and a round-towered church.

There are seven South Elmhams. In woods near **St Margaret South Elmham** lie medieval ruins of the Minster, which possibly replaced a Saxon minster built when the bishopric of Elmham was founded in AD 675 and linked to Dunwich. Claims for the site of a great Saxon cathedral are disputed with North Elmham in Norfolk. Many of the churches in these groups of villages were built by Normans.

In the locality: Mettingham Castle, page 77; Norfolk and Suffolk Aviation Museum, page 104; Otter Trust, page 122; St Cross Farm Walks, page 67; and church at Barsham with Shipmeadow, page 80.

Saxmundham
OS 156: TM 385632. Population 2620.
Early closing Thursday; market day Wednesday.

Saxmundham is a small market town in the valley of the river Fromus, a tributary of the Alde. A Saxon settlement, with three churches by Domesday, its market was granted in 1272 and a position on the road from Ipswich to Great Yarmouth ensured it was an early mail-coach stop.

The town expanded further in the early nineteenth century. In 1846 the Corn Exchange was completed with a stucco arcade displaying the arms of the Longs of nearby Hurts Hall. The railway arrived thirteen years later, providing links with Aldeburgh and Thorpeness (for holidays) and Leiston (for industry); railway workers' dwellings remain in Albion Street. The railway also brought in white bricks, resulting in many High Street buildings being refronted.

In the locality: Bruisyard Wines, page 120; George E. Cook, basketmaker, page 115; the Long Shop Museum, page 106; church at Leiston, page 90.

Saxtead Green

Saxtead Green Post Mill, page 117.

Shotley Peninsula

Around OS 169: TM 220360.

This is the area between the rivers Orwell and Stour. Offshore are busy shipping lanes from which huge vessels converge on the container and passenger terminals at Felixstowe, Harwich, Parkeston Quay and Ipswich.

Overlooking Harwich Harbour, **Shotley Point** is sometimes called the Bloody Point, where King Alfred's fleet saw off Danish marauders in AD 855. Small villages overlook the estuaries, typical settlements being Stutton, Woolverstone and Shotley Gate. The countryside undulates, containing the man-made reservoir of **Alton Water** with its perimeter walk, nature reserve and visitor centre. Another point of interest is the Royal Hospital School, founded in Greenwich in 1694 and moved to **Holbrook** in 1935. Its formally planned village is dominated by a 200 feet (60 metres) high clock-tower, recalling the mast of HMS *Ganges.*

Shotley Peninsula offers some architectural curiosities. The gateway to **Erwarton Hall**, built in 1549, is a rich red-brick Jacobean fantasy with pinnacles like chimneys (OS 169: TM 224352). In contrast, **Freston Tower** was raised six storeys high just a few years later for Hugh de Freston, reputedly providing his daughter with a different schoolroom for each weekday, but more likely so that he could watch shipping in the river. Finally, **Tattingstone Wonder** (1770) was built to appear like a church when seen from the big house (the squire's wife, an invalid, wanted to see one), but it is a sham, accommodating three cottages for farmworkers (OS 169: TM 139363).

In the locality: Freston Woods, page 64;

Left: *The Jacobean gatehouse at Erwarton Hall on the Shotley Peninsula.*

Right: *Built to look like a church from the front, the Tattingstone Wonder is a famous eyecatcher.*

Heather and the coastguard cottages on Dunwich Heath.

Elaborate wall decoration on the Ancient House in the Buttermarket, Ipswich.

The Deanery and parish church at Hadleigh.

HMS Ganges Association Museum, page 108.

Sibton

See Peasenhall, page 39.

Sizewell

Sizewell Visitor Centre, page 118.

Snape

OS 156: TM 395583. Population 620.
Snape is a tiny port on the small tidal river Alde. Low ebb is a mere trickle; high tide brings enough brackish water to float a sailing barge along the quay, from where superb views extend to the horizon over reedbeds, creeks and saltmarsh.

Snape Maltings expanded through the Victorian era to become one of the largest in East Anglia. Part of the mellow granaries and malthouses was converted in 1967 into Aldeburgh Festival's concert hall, but it caught fire on the opening night, was enthusiastically rebuilt and reopened in 1970 to become internationally famous. The acoustic excellence of the warm red-brick interior and

Snape church.

its timbered roof encourages year-round concerts, especially in April (Early Music Festival), June (Aldeburgh Festival), August (Snape Proms) and October (Britten Festival). Other parts of the Maltings house the Britten-Pears School for Advanced Musical Studies and the diverse craft shops and galleries of Snape Maltings Riverside Centre (telephone: 01728 688303).

In the locality: Blaxhall Common, page 61; George E. Cook, basketmaker, page 115; Iken Cliff, page 65; Moot Hall Museum, page 102; church at Leiston, page 90.

Somerleyton

Somerleyton Hall, page 100.

Southwold

OS 156: TM 509763. Population 4050.
Southwold was prosperous by the 1550s from shipbuilding and fishing, Buss Creek being home to herring 'busses'. Difficulties in maintaining the harbour resulted in a new cut to the sea in the 1590s. In 1659 a great fire destroyed the town hall, jail and 238 dwellings; subsequent rebuilding created

The Sole Bay Inn and the lighthouse at Southwold.

nine greens which give today's town its spacious character. Near Bartholomew Green, curious carved heads are painted on numbers 31-7 St Edmund's Terrace. East Green is dominated by the smooth white lighthouse built in 1890 and is also the site of Adnam's brewery, whose Sole Bay Inn overlooks St James Green. South Green is the largest; it hosts Trinity Fair.

From 1740 there were attempts to establish in Southwold a Free British Fishery to challenge the Dutch monopoly of the North Sea herring fishing grounds. The proposals encouraged various developments and in 1746 six eighteen-pounder guns on carriages were presented to the town (possibly dating from 1485 and captured at Culloden); Southwold was bombarded in the First World War because they were deemed a fortification, so the guns were buried in the Second World War and now occupy Gun Hill, where there was already a battery at the time of the Armada in 1588.

Southwold is full of eclectic buildings recalling its Regency days as a fashionable watering place or later ventures such as the Edwardian School of Industrial Art in Park Lane. The town has a pleasant, light-hearted atmosphere and it is easily explored, offering good views in and out largely unspoilt by

Woodbridge Shire Hall.

suburbs, for on three sides are creeks, marshes and the river Blyth. From above the short pier over the stony beach a clifftop walk passes beach-huts and a rigged mast and cannon. Another quarter of the town overlooks the Common and on, beyond, to the forceful river Blyth, the harbour and Walberswick; the two curious water towers date from 1886 and 1937.

The central triangular Market Place, on the site of the former market cross, is dominated by the lovely iron sign of the Swan Hotel, adjacent to the town hall and tourist information centre, which displays tide tables. The nearby town pump, cast in 1873, is decorated with herrings, dolphins and the crown and arrows of St Edmund.

Church of St Edmund, page 94; **Sailors' Reading Room**, page 108; **Southwold Lifeboat Museum**, page 108; **Southwold Museum**, page 108;

In the locality: Benacre National Nature Reserve, page 61; Henham Walks, page 64; Norman Gwatkin, page 66; Reydon Wood, page 67; Suffolk Heritage Coast Path, page 68; Walberswick National Nature Reserve, page 69; Wrentham Basketware, page 118; and churches at Blythburgh, page 80; Covehithe, page 82; and Walberswick, page 94.

Southwold's famous Swan Hotel.

Stanton
Stanton Rides, page 67; Stanton Windmill, page 118; Wyken Hall Gardens and Vineyards, page 121.

Stoke by Clare
OS 155: TL 742435.
Stoke by Clare is an attractive village with a duck pond and two greens connected by a broad main street full of thatched houses – many colourwashed, pargeted, jetted and pegtiled – with a few handsome Georgian brick frontages. The village sign is on the smaller green, screened by horse-chestnut trees from St John's church, which contains a tiny pulpit only 28 inches (71 cm) in diameter and stained glass from 1480 depicting a windmill. Beside the green is a fine early six-teenth-century dovecote built of red and blue bricks laid into patterns which include a portcullis. There is also a Gothick flint gate-lodge serving the distant Stoke College, which is now a school but around 1090 was a Benedictine priory linked with Bec in Normandy, converted to a college of seculars in 1415.

Boyton Vineyard, page 120.

In the locality: Clare Castle, page 75; Clare Country Park, page 62; Clare Priory, page 75.

Stoke-by-Nayland
See Nayland, page 35.

Stonham Aspal
British Birds of Prey and Conservation Centre, page 122; Mickfield Meadow, page 66.

Stowlangtoft
Church of St George, page 94.

Stowmarket
OS 155: TM 050585. Population 13,600.
Early closing Tuesday; market days
Thursday and Saturday.

At the geographical centre of the county, amidst agricultural prosperity, Stowmarket is a High Suffolk market town bordered by the rivers Gipping and Rat. In 1348 the town and manor were granted to the Austin Abbots of St Osyth, who supervised its market, chartered in 1387, and whose tithe barn partly survives. The biggest fillip to growth was the completion in 1793 of the river Gipping navigation, bringing major expansion and an industrial link to Ipswich. There followed the construction of numerous maltings and a highly successful ironworks. The railway arrived in 1846, celebrated in a dramatic station with ornamental brick gateways and octagonal towers, and Stowmarket remained geographically significant on the main road to the Midlands until bypassed in the 1970s.

Stowmarket's early chemical industry produced a guncotton works in 1863. One setback occurred when it blew up in 1871, killing twenty-eight people. The works was rebuilt, manufacturing cordite in 1878; the workforce reached two thousand during the First World War. Since the Second World War a number of specialised factories have been set up, including one of Europe's major paint-producing plants.

Alton Watermill, page 117; **Eastbridge Windpump**, page 117; **Museum of East Anglian Life**, page 108.

In the locality: British Birds of Prey and Conservation Centre, page 122; Combs Wood, page 62; Fen Alder Carr, page 63; Gipping Valley River Path, page 64; Haughley Park, page 98; Mechanical Music Museum Trust, page 103; Mickfield Meadow, page 66; Mid Suffolk Footpath, page 66; Mid-Suffolk Light Railway Society Museum, page 109; Northfield Wood, page 66; Wattisham Airfield Historical Collection, page 109; Woolpit and District Museum, page 110; and churches at Great Finborough, page 83; Gipping, page 83; Needham Market, page 91.

Sudbury
OS 155: TL 875415. Population 19,520.
Market days Thursday and Saturday.

Sudbury stands on high defensible ground in a loop of the river Stour, comparable with Bungay on the Waveney. The early moated Saxon town (on the site of today's School Street) grew with wealth from the cloth industry. Religious orders are recalled by Blackfriars Street and at the priory gatehouse of a vanished Dominican friary founded before 1248.

After medieval prosperity, Sudbury continued to expand, concentrating on silks, velvets and fine hangings. Thus its Tudor buildings were updated with wharves, warehouses and a navigable waterway to Manningtree. Along Quay Lane, overlooking The Basin, are later, muscular brick industrial waterfront buildings with semicircular windows, like Quay Theatre and The Granary, home of the River Stour Trust.

The statue of Thomas Gainsborough in front of St Peter's church on Sudbury's Market Hill.

Dominating the central triangular Market Hill is the redundant church of St Peter with its tower completed by 1475. It looks over an ebullient white Tuscan-columned library, formerly the Corn Exchange built in 1841, and the 1913 statue of Thomas Gainsborough (1727-88), Sudbury's most famous son. Below, Friars Street includes larger Georgian-fronted dwellings and former clothiers' houses such as Buzzard's Hall. Stour Street retains substantial medieval carved and closely timber-studded houses such as The Chantry and Salter's Hall. These lead down to the former watermill, now an hotel, from where there is good access to Sudbury Common Lands (a Site of Special Scientific Interest). There, footpaths extend over 115 acres (47 hectares) of river Stour floodplain, including water-meadows grazed continuously since 1086, the rights passing in 1260 from Richard de Clare to the burgesses and freemen of Sudbury, one of whom in a later century was Thomas Gainsborough's father.

Church of St Gregory on the Croft, page 94; **Gainsborough's House**, page 109; **Gainsborough Silk Weaving Company**, page 115.

In the locality, Arger Fen, page 61; Cornard Mere, page 63; Kentwell Hall, page 99; Melford Hall, page 99; and churches at Boxford, page 80; and Long Melford, page 90.

Sutton

Sutton Heath and Common, page 68; Sutton Hoo, page 71.

Thelnetham

Thelnetham Fen, page 68; Thelnetham Windmill, page 118.

Thornham Magna

Thornham Walks, page 69.

Thorpeness

OS 156: TM 474598.

Thorpeness is a distinctively themed seaside village built in 1910-40 around a 65 acre (26 hectare) lake converted to The Mere, an escapist's delight of small boats and little islands, many recalling the story of Peter Pan. J. M. Barrie's friend Stuart Ogilvie was responsible, building groups of asymmetric dwellings, black and white boarded, with balconies and unusual chimneys. A windmill was brought in to pump water to the bizarre House in the Clouds, now a residence atop sixty-eight winding steps, which lives up to its name. A second water tower, the West Bar, is disguised as a Tudor gatehouse, built in 1928. Other curious buildings include the almshouses, the country club, a golf clubhouse with huge decorative tees on its roof and a remarkably solid-looking church. Hidden away are some tiny tarred wooden dwellings.

The Haven, page 64; **Thorpeness Post Mill**, page 118.

In the locality: the Long Shop Museum, page 106; Moot Hall Museum, page 102; North Warren, page 67; Sizewell Visitor Centre, page 118; Suffolk Heritage Coast Path, page 68; and church at Leiston, page 90.

Trimley St Mary

Trimley Marshes, page 69.

Ufford

OS 156: TM 298524. Population 810.

Ufford is believed to be named as a ford of the Wuffings, the royal house associated with Sutton Hoo. A small picturesque village of colourwashed and thatched houses, it is surrounded by water-meadows screened by willows and poplars. Near the almshouses of 1690, beside the whipping post and stocks, is Ufford's church, renowned for its elaborately carved telescopic font cover which extends, in tiers of finials, right up to the church roof, making it perhaps the tallest in England.

In the locality: Bromeswell Green and Wilford Bridge, page 62; Buttrum's Mill, page 115; Suffolk Horse Museum, page 110; Valley Farm Camargue Horses and White Animal Collection, page 123; Woodbridge Museum, page 110; Woodbridge Tide Mill, page 118; and church at Woodbridge, page 95.

Walberswick

OS 156: TM 495747. Population 460.

This calm village is approached across open heathland or by ferry or footbridge from Southwold; it lies between the river Blyth and Sole Bay. In the early twentieth century Walberswick's ambience attracted a painting

The ferry from Walberswick to Southwold.

colony of artists including Charles Rennie Mackintosh, 'Glasgow Boy' Edward Arthur Walton, Stanley Spencer and also Philip Wilson Steer (1860-1942), the leading 'English Impressionist', who painted dreamy pictures of Walberswick's gentle sandy beaches using flecked brush strokes and sparkling colours. Intellectuals came too, so the resort was nicknamed Hampstead-on-Sea. Now it is better known for its national crabbing contest each August.

Real prosperity came much earlier: from 1350 there was trade in butter, bacon, corn, fish and shipbuilding – in 1451 extending as far afield as Iceland and the Faeroes. The town suffered from storms in the same way as nearby Dunwich, so in 1590 its river was linked to Southwold, the new outlet being cut 3 miles (5 km) further north than the old one. Since the 1650s Walberswick has looked backwards; now a muddy creek replaces Dunwich Haven.

A stroll through the village from the ferry leads past Fishermen's Flats, where nets are dried. The views are over riverside impedimenta: tarred and bleached wooden huts and people messing about in boats. Much of the pebble, brick and flint village lies around the main green, where a late Victorian Congregational chapel houses a Heritage Coast Centre. **Church of St Andrew**, page 94; **Walberswick National Nature Reserve**, page 69.

In the locality: Dunwich Greyfriars, page 75; Dunwich Museum, page 104; Southwold Lifeboat Museum, page 108; Southwold Museum, page 108; Southwold Sailors' Reading Room, page 108; Suffolk Heritage Coast Path, page 68; Toby's Walks, page 69; Westleton Heath, page 69; and churches at Blythburgh, page 80; and Southwold, page 94.

Walsham le Willows

OS 144, 155: TM 005713. Population 1010.
The village enjoys a good mixture of boarded and colourwashed houses interspersed with village shops and pubs, all extending several hundred yards along the main street. A stream runs part of the way, which is best walked from St Mary's church with its pollarded trees to the flint-built mill at Wattisfield Road. There are some splendid old houses on the village periphery.

In the locality: Bardwell Windmill, page

114; Market Weston Fen, page 66; Mechanical Music Museum Trust, page 103; Redgrave and Lopham Fens National Nature Reserve, page 67; Stanton Rides, page 67; Stanton Windmill, page 118; Thelnetham Fen, page 68; Thelnetham Windmill, page 118; Wyken Hall Gardens and Vineyards, page 121; churches at Stowlangtoft, page 94; and Wortham, page 95.

Wenhaston

Church of St Peter, page 94.

Westleton

OS 156: TM 441691. Population 480.
Surrounding Westleton's sloping triangular green are unassuming terraced cottages, tiled and colourwashed or built of angular ochre pebbles quoined in white brick. There are some fine trellised porches and curios – and unexpected backstreet pargeting. Near the square duck pond, or Green Ditch, are village pumps, pubs, a Victorian school and the Witches' Stone. A hurricane destroyed the church tower in 1776 and its timber replacement was later hit by a bomb. On the village perimeter lie Georgian houses, a famous clematis nursery, then wooded heathland.
Westleton Heath National Nature Reserve, page 69.

In the locality: Darsham Marshes, page 63; Dunwich Greyfriars, page 75; Dunwich Heath and Dunwich Common, page 63; Dunwich Museum, page 104; Minsmere Nature Reserve, page 66; Sizewell Visitor Centre, page 118; and church at Leiston, page 90.

Weston

Winter Flora, page 123.

West Stow

Anglo-Saxon Village, page 71; Cow Wise, page 120; West Stow Country Park, page 69.

Wetheringsett

Mid-Suffolk Light Railway Society Museum, page 109.

Wickham Market

OS 156: TM 302558. Population 2200.
Bypassed by the A12, this quiet village with its tall-spired church and little square was granted a market about 1440 under Henry VI. In the 1730s John Kirby wrote his influential *Suffolk Traveller* here and in the following century a watermill on the river Deben and a foundry were established.
Valley Farm Camargue Horses and White Animal Collection, page 123.

In the locality: Akenfield, page 97; Easton Farm Park, page 120; Letheringham Watermill, page 116; Otley Hall, page 100; 390th Bomb Group Memorial Air Museum, page 108; and church at Woodbridge, page 95.

Wingfield

Church of St Andrew, page 95; Wingfield Old College and Gardens, page 101.

Woodbridge

OS 169: TM 270490. Population 7670.
Early closing Wednesday; market day Thursday.
Woodbridge is an attractive market town and former port to one side of the tidal river Deben. The surroundings are heathland, water-meadows, farms and forest. There is no wooden bridge; the name relates to 'Woden's town' and medieval prosperity was based on shipbuilding and trade.

Benefactors of the town have included Thomas Seckford (1515-87), who was Master of the Rolls at Queen Elizabeth I's court (his brother was a pirate). He is credited with commissioning the Shire Hall around 1575 on the central Market Hill, a building which marked the replacement of Wickham Market by Woodbridge as a regional centre. Greatly remodelled, the Shire Hall later acquired Dutch gables, stone stairs, lock-up cells and the court room of the Liberty of St Etheldreda. Adjacent, behind the Victorian pump, stands the King's Head pub. It was once the guildhall and its carved heads lead into cosmopolitan Seckford Street, where around 1840 Thomas Seckford's legacy built the splendid arcaded Seckford Hospital.

From Market Hill, the town's commercial centre is reached down either Church Street or New Street (new in 1550), passing the Steelyard, an apparatus once used to weigh wagonloads of corn, last operated in 1880.

Next door are the sixteenth-century Bell and Steelyard pub and the Bridewell or former jail. The gently curving Thoroughfare with its many shops was once part of the main Ipswich to Lowestoft road; Elmhurst Park separates it from the river Deben quayside with its marina, boatyards and the riverside footpath from Ferry Quay to Kyson Hill (National Trust) and Martlesham Creek, opposite Sutton Hoo. The Thoroughfare continues into prosperous Cumberland Street, full of imposing Georgian houses which date from Woodbridge's period as a Napoleonic garrison town for officers.

Buttrum's Mill, page 115; **church of St Mary**, page 95; **Suffolk Horse Museum**, page 110; **Woodbridge Museum**, page 110; **Woodbridge Tide Mill**, page 118.

In the locality: Akenfield, page 97; Bromeswell Green and Wilford Bridge, page 62; Butley Priory Gatehouse, page 75; Newbourne Springs, page 66; Otley Hall, page 100; Rendlesham Forest, page 67; Seckford Hall, page 100; Simpson's Saltings, page 67; Staverton Thicks, page 68; Sutton Heath and Common, page 68; Sutton Hoo, page 71; Tang Valley Trail, page 68; Valley Farm Camargue Horses and White Animal Collection, page 123.

Woolpit

OS 155: TL 975624. Population 1660.

The town is named from Saxon wolf-trapping pits, but clay pits were also dug for brickmaking; durable 'Woolpit Whites', available by 1692, reached their greatest output from 1850 to 1930. The town hosted an important cattle fair until the nineteenth century (Cow Fair is now a street) and as early as 1557 it was reputedly one of the four best horse and colt markets in England.

The town centre is a triangular crossroads around the conical-roofed pavilion of the Well of Remembrance to Queen Victoria. Overlooking it is the conspicuous spire of St Mary's church and a pleasant collection of pubs and old houses.

Just outside the village is the ancient Lady's Well, also known as Palgress, to which medieval pilgrims came to bathe their eyes and pray to Our Lady. More a moat-like excavation than a well, it is perhaps an early defensive site though medicinal qualities were attributed to the high sulphate content of the water.

Documents from about 1400 record the discovery in a Woolpit harvest field of two green-skinned children with white hair who spoke a strange language. They were adopted by the village.

Woolpit and District Museum, page 110.

In the locality: Haughley Park, page 98; Netherfield Herb Garden, page 122; Pakenham Watermill, page 117; and churches at Hessett, page 86; and Stowlangtoft, page 94.

Wortham

Church of St Mary, page 95; Wortham Ling, page 69.

Wrentham

Wrentham Basketware, page 118.

Yoxford

OS 156: TM 394690. Population 810. Early closing Wednesday; market day Friday.

Yoxford was a major coaching halt on the London to Great Yarmouth route before the railway arrived. Thus it is no surprise to find by the lead-spired St Peter's church an iron signpost cast around 1830 to 'Yarmouth, Framlingham and London' and Milestone House with its Regency balcony. Yoxford calls itself the 'Garden of Suffolk' and has built up an attractive main street on the site of a Roman road, especially between the Primitive Methodist chapel and the thatched bus shelter. The village is surrounded by the parkland of three country houses, including Cockfield Hall, where a sister of Lady Jane Grey was confined on the orders of Queen Elizabeth I.

In the locality: Darsham Marshes, page 63; and church at Bramfield, page 80.

3
Coast and countryside

Suffolk's geology is varied. In the west chalk rises to the surface and thin soils on it contrast with black fenland or merge into sandy Breckland. To the east, bordering the Sandlings, the remains of old seabeds provide soft crumbly cliffs of crag or shelly sand. In southern Suffolk London clay spills over from Essex into the lower river valleys. Across Suffolk, from south-west to north-east, broad belts of stiff stony boulder clay provide deep and fertile soils. The highest point in the county is only 110 metres (400 feet) above sea level; the valleys and low wetlands are rich in peat and alluvium.

Until the twentieth century the Suffolk countryside was farmed according to its natural characteristics. Land reclamation in the fens and coastal marshes since medieval times and a progression from seventeenth-century dairying to early twentieth-century arable farming had none of the impact on the landscape achieved by post-war agribusiness. That transformed, for example, traditional sheep-grazed chalk downland into profitable cornfields from Bury St Edmunds to Newmarket. All around, the cultivation of heavy clay soils was revolutionised by the use of mechanical equipment which maximised crop yield whilst sacrificing hedges, destroying the old mosaic patterns of fields and introducing chemical sprays. Inevitably, copses and flower meadows suffered badly and ditches, streams, water-meadows and lush cow pasture were removed. In a similar way, the widespread introduction of irrigation, fertilisers and plastic sheeting to the Sandlings has changed that area too, though since the 1920s new conifer plantations have been taking over the open heaths, hiding their sheepwalks and rabbit warrens, whilst providing shelter and contrast. The extensive post-war drainage of coastal marshes and fenland and the construction of flood protection dykes were further attempts to produce arable prairies. Thus natural contrasts in the countryside have become blurred, particularly between heavy clay areas and the lighter Sandlings and Breckland.

The individual character of these areas had been defined over centuries through interactions of local industry, agriculture and economics. Thus there was a correlation between timber-framed construction and managed oak woodland, between grazing flocks and heathland, between thatched roofs and reedbeds or cornfields. That relationship has largely gone yet much of the Suffolk coastland and countryside remains particularly beautiful.

The shore and coastline

Some 50 miles (80 km) of coastline run from north to south in a mix of sand, shingle, salt-marsh and estuary, mostly protected both as Heritage Coast and as an Area of Outstanding Natural Beauty.

The moody dominant North Sea is always changing. Motionless and blue on summer days, glistening and serene, it easily turns to murky breakers and in medieval times destroyed the city of Dunwich. This coastline has shrunk and grown; rivers have altered their course; towns have lost their fortunes as ports silted up; marsh has become farmland and later returned to the seabed. The greatest recent flood was in 1953 and that generated many of the sea defence measures in evidence today. Bathing off these beaches can be hazardous because of strong undertows and steep shelves.

Sandy cliffs of orange-brown or red crag, some with good fossil beds, have eroded spectacularly at Dunwich; at Covehithe the old road literally goes over the cliff. Such cliffs drop sheer to the beach and may slump without warning, uprooting trees and leaving pathways severed in mid air. Once fallen, the sand becomes dunes and foreshore, accreting further along the coast or contributing to sandy shoals just offshore. Benacre Ness and Easton

Bavents are the sites of ancient submerged forest, the former providing the bog-oak used for fittings now on display at Southwold Town Hall.

Sandy beaches are outnumbered by beaches of pebbles, which range through glistening ochres and blues, in size from grit to paperweight, crunching as one beachcombs for amber, jet, bloodstone or unusual driftwood. From gentle inclines, one storm can dramatically sculpt steep terraces overnight. Extensive, curved sweeps of pebble beach, as near Aldeburgh and Bawdsey, appear more spectacular when first covered by a fresh fall of snow.

The intertidal zone reveals seaweeds, starfish, whelk egg-cases and assorted wave-driven detritus. Just above this zone is sufficient nourishment for salt-loving plants like sea campion, sea lavender, sea lupin, sea holly and yellow horned poppy; one may also find the beach-nesting ringed plover.

Estuaries

Shelter is provided and ribbon development along the coast blocked by five notable Suffolk estuaries which empty the Stour, Orwell, Deben, Alde/Ore/Butley and Blyth into the North Sea. Previous estuaries have been closed by the longshore drift of shingle bars, creating marshy nesses such as Benacre Broad and Minsmere, or closing rivers like the Hundred near Aldeburgh. From medieval times, the silting up of harbours through longshore drift, together with the increasing draught of ships, brought the closure of ports like Orford, Dunwich and Blythburgh.

Each Suffolk estuary has a different character; all are popular with sailors and important for wildfowl. They originate in pastoral upper reaches, from where streams and brooks run through villages and reedbeds into creeks where low tides reveal expanses of shiny, glutinous, smoothly contoured mudflats supporting wading birds and the angled hulls of pleasure boats. These mudflats are full of food for wading birds but exposed for a few hours only; then the high-brimming tide returns to reflect the changing light of Suffolk's vast skies.

The estuaries of the Orwell and Stour are large and straight, with steeper wooded slopes

and historic estates; those of the Deben and Blyth are more sinuous and shallow. A good way to see the estuaries is by boat and organised trips and boat hire are available from Bungay, Orford, Oulton Broad, Southwold, Snape Maltings, Sudbury and Waldringfield.

Estuarine rivers

The river Stour

Rising from three sources, one in Suffolk at Kedington and two in Essex, the Stour is the longest East Anglian river. It runs 50 miles (80 km), fed by important tributaries like the Glem, Box and Brett through the cloth towns of Clare, Cavendish and Long Melford. The Stour was the first local river to be uprated to a navigation, in 1714 reaching Sudbury. From there the Stour swells, forming a flood plain at Dedham Vale, passing Flatford Mill and widening further beside Manningtree. Soon it is 2 miles (3 km) across, the greatest, broadest, straightest Suffolk estuary – albeit the southern shore is Essex – flowing to meet the Orwell in Harwich Harbour below Shotley Gate. Its south-facing shore has attracted many fine houses and well-appointed villages such as Harkstead.

The river Gipping or Orwell

The Gipping rises at Mendlesham Green, passing through rich agricultural land around Stowmarket and powering watermills at Needham Market and Sproughton. Bypassing the docks, it meets Ipswich at New Cut, rapidly expanding as it becomes the Orwell, a sizeable working river with waterfront, marinas and dock facilities. Beyond the dramatic concrete sweep of the Orwell Bridge (opened 1982) the banks become rural again; at Nacton the sandy seaweeded foreshore is littered with tree roots exposed by high tides. Just across the river is The Strand (English Nature) with its saltmarsh, leading into Chelmondiston and picturesque Pin Mill. Here are boatyards, a cliff owned by the National Trust and the Butt and Oyster pub, licensed in 1553, overlooking a muddy river shore with an array of houseboats and assorted pleasure craft. Larger ships chug upstream to Ipswich. This is the territory of Arthur Ransome's novels like *We Didn't Mean to Go to Sea*, where Thames

At Covehithe the steep, sandy cliff continually breaks away on to the beach.

barges were built and return to race each June. The broad river flows between gently wooded slopes separated by small tributaries, mudflats and marshland, with marinas at Woolverstone and Levington and the designed landscape of Orwell Park. Between Felixstowe and Harwich, at Shotley Point, the Orwell meets the Stour and both enter the North Sea.

The river Deben

The Deben rises appropriately near Debenham and flows to Brandeston, where it broadens past Letheringham's watermill, through the water-meadows of villages like Easton and Ufford. By the boatyards and slipways of Woodbridge and its famous tide mill, below Sutton Hoo, the Deben grows into a proper tidal river full of pleasure craft which navigate its gentle curves to snug, popular havens with lovely river views like Waldringfield and Ramsholt. After a section of marshland, the Deben squeezes through the narrow channel of Felixstowe Ferry to debouch into open sea.

The river Alde or Ore

The Alde rises at Brundish, trickling past Bruisyard, Rendham and Farnham. At Snape bridge, beside the Maltings, it becomes a tidal river, widening into reedbeds and muddy openness below Iken's south bank, where St Botolph's monastery was established in AD 654. Then come the broad Long Reach and a lazy meander past Cob Island to the silhouette of picturesque conifers called 'Little Japan', near Aldeburgh, where it all but runs into the North Sea. Sea defences ensure that it does not: they came after the township of Slaughden was washed away. From this point the long shingle spit of Orford Ness with its lighthouse extends southwards. In this last stretch, past Havergate Island, the Alde becomes the Ore and it finally joins the sea near Hollesley.

An assortment of pleasure craft at Pin Mill on the river Orwell.

The river Blyth

The Blyth rises at Laxfield, was once forded by the old Roman road at Ubbeston, then passes Huntingfield with its hall and the Queen's Oak. It widens into a lake in the landscaped grounds of Heveningham Hall, to flow on past Walpole and Halesworth, where tributaries join from the Saints country. Beyond Wenhaston the Blyth swells into a huge expanse of muddiness or reflected sky, depending on the tide. Overlooking it is the magnificent church of Blythburgh and its tiny village, once a town with a mint and a jail. Then it is only a short distance to the sea, where the river surges past boating paraphernalia between Southwold and Walberswick, surrounded by marshes. The Blyth once entered the sea at Dunwich.

The river Waveney

At the north edge of Suffolk, the Waveney defines much of the border with Norfolk. It rises at South Lopham, on the Suffolk side skirting Hoxne and Mendham, and loops protectively around Bungay and Beccles, where it supports boatbuilders and river cruisers.

Out of the town the river almost loses itself in a huge expanse of marshland, some of which discharges water to the sea through Oulton Broad, Lake Lothing and Lowestoft, before it rallies and crosses the county boundary in the direction of Great Yarmouth, the Yare and Breydon Water.

River valleys

Suffolk's marine boundary is supplemented by the Waveney to the north, the Stour to the south and the Linnet and Lark to the west. Numerous associated tributaries run in a network of valleys including the Yox or Min, the Dove, Fynn and Mill, two river Hundreds, the Glem, Brett, Box and Chad Brook. Dedham Vale is the product of the river Stour. Towns, villages and watermills grew on these streams and rivers, some of which became navigations for the export of farm products and the import of bricks and coal. In open country, lower areas periodically flood into lush water-meadows traditionally grazed by red poll cattle against a characteristic backdrop of osier, alder, willow and poplar.

Marshland, broads and fenland

Suffolk marshland varies from saltmarsh to freshwater. Much of it, like water-meadows, provided traditional grazing for sheep and cattle, growing lush grass from rich alluvium which periodically disappears under flood water. Sometimes this happened on a grand scale: coastal areas were purposefully flooded around 1940 to discourage the possibility of invasion, and an inundation by the sea in 1953 disrupted much of the east coast, drowning livestock and over three hundred people.

From Norman times there have been attempts to reclaim marshland for year-round cultivation. After 1953 protective earth dykes were raised and great acreages of wetland drained, altering both landscape and water table. In some ways that has been seen to be environmentally unsatisfactory, so landowners are letting water levels rise once again, recreating marshland and water-meadows.

On the coast saltmarsh nourishes glasswort, thrift, sea aster, sea lavender, sea purslane, sea blite, rice grass and marsh samphire (or poor man's asparagus) at places like Greenfield Bay and Hemley. Where the terrain is even wetter, saline meres are formed, as at Covehithe, Easton Broads and Benacre. Benacre Broad has its own 'Bay of Biscay'. There are also true broads like Fritton Lake, Flixton Decoy and Barnby Broad, wetland areas of rivers, dykes and shallow lakes affected by medieval turbary or peat extraction. In 1318 76 per cent of the total income of Fritton Manor came from peat cutting; in 1341 present-day Oulton Broad apparently exported 300,000 turves, mostly for fuel. More recently created coastal lagoons between Walberswick and Shingle Street indicate where mud has been extracted to build sea defences.

There is extensive freshwater marshland, especially beside the river Waveney; such areas support birdlife including snipe, wigeon, shoveller, gadwall, sedge warbler, treecreeper, marsh and bearded tits and marsh harrier. Typical flora includes marsh marigold, bog pimpernel, marsh orchid and extensive reedbeds.

Reeds prefer a constant water depth of 4 inches (10 cm), but without active management (stimulated for example by the thatching industry) reedbeds are prone to dry out, filling with leaves and scrub, and eventually becoming woodland. Winter reed cutting improves the seed heads; this stimulates other growth like sedges, attracting dragonflies and bitterns. Where rush and sedge grow below a tree canopy, the resulting habitat is termed alder or willow carr.

Large areas of former fenland have been drained since the eighteenth century and to the west, in the Lakenheath-Newmarket-Mildenhall triangle, lie areas of true peatland. The landscape is flat, near sea level, offering long geometric views down straight roads. The high fertility of the silty black soil encourages intensive farming and fields are bordered not by hedges but with dykes, flood relief channels and drainage ditches. Settlements like Sedge Fen are small and isolated, sparse hamlets and collections of farm buildings being sheltered by precise rows of poplars.

The central clay area of High Suffolk

A large part of Suffolk – at least half, centred on Bury St Edmunds – is covered with heavy boulder clay, or till. This was deposited by retreating glaciers, together with layers of flint and chalk, to form a gently rolling landscape. Considerable areas were covered in oak forest, which was gradually felled to become fields that now grow corn and sugar beet. Thus many place-names end in '-field', recording ancient forest clearings. Boulder clay is demanding agricultural land, glutinous in winter, holding standing water, thus requiring deep drainage ditches. Then the summer sun bakes it hard and unyielding. So farmers have brought in heavy agricultural machinery, which, having created huge fields, has generated immense crop yields. In spite of this, extensive woodlands remain.

Years ago, villagers used their clay wisely. In medieval times scores of wonderful houses in High Suffolk were moated in imitation of defensive earthworks, probably more to impress than to defend. Such excavations yielded material which was either used to infill timber-framed walls or dried into clay lump for building with. When the moat filled with water it supported fish. Encouraged by the landscape movement, some larger moats in the grounds of country houses were later converted to reflecting pools and even ornamental canals.

The Sandlings

The Sandlings were once extensive sandy coastal heathlands stretching from Ipswich to Lowestoft. For centuries they were cropped by rabbits and by sheep which followed 'walks' to reach richer grazing in the river valleys. It is estimated that since 1900 80 per cent of this habitat has been ploughed up or forested with conifers; much has been modified to encourage carrots and early potatoes and to rear pigs and pheasants.

What remains of the Sandlings is all east of the A12, and much is now protected. Left ungrazed, it risks colonisation by invasive pine and birch trees. Where the ground cover is disturbed, sandstorms frequently result.

The acid soils nourish varied grasses, ling and sand sedge, whilst sandy tracks may redden with mossy tillaea. Summer brings a rich clash of yellow and purple from the blossoming gorse and heather; winter rains render it a sodden raw umber, contrasting with the soft orange of dead bracken and straw-coloured grasses. Lizards, adders, nightjars and woodlarks make their homes here. Heathland moths include the grass wave, black rustic and deep brown dart.

Breckland

Breckland extends around Brandon across both Suffolk and Norfolk. The area is a huge inland sand dune lying over solid chalk rich in flint beds; this arrangement has produced a range of special soils which, along with low rainfall, unpredictable frosts, cold winters and dry summers, has created a unique habitat.

Clearance of the scattered woodland began around 3000 BC, leading to dense settlement of the land. The settlers seem to have exhausted the poor soil, leaving behind them steppe-like dry grass heaths called 'brecks', along with abandoned flint mines and burial mounds, especially bronze age barrows.

Like the Sandlings, the Breckland heaths were for centuries – perhaps since neolithic

times – cropped by goats and sheep. Then following the Norman conquest they were nibbled by farmed rabbits; 'warren' place-names are numerous.

Where the light soil is disturbed, sandstorms can result; indeed, Santon Downham was buried in a seventeenth-century 'sand flood' such as that described by John Evelyn in 1667: 'the Travelling Sands...that have so damaged the country, rouling from place to place, and like the Sands in the deserts of Lybia, quite overwhelmed some gentlemen's whole estates'. Since the eighteenth century Scots pines have been planted to stabilise the sand, joined in the 1920s by extensive afforestation with Corsican pine.

Many Breckland plants thrive on the disturbance brought by shifting sands. Dry habitats support biting stonecrop, centaury, cudweed and stork's-bill. Wetter areas attract ferns, reeds, water mint and iris. Also present are Spanish catchfly, dense silky-bent, toadflax, corn camomile and flixweed. Breckland birds include the stone curlew, wheatear, crossbill, red-backed shrike, woodlark and nightjar.

Grassland and meadows

Mid Suffolk's dairy boom around 1800 helped create many flower-rich meadows. All over Suffolk water-meadows, hay meadows, commons, greens, churchyards and even roadside verges are abundant with varied flowers and plant life. Naturally there is greatest interest in areas which have been least disturbed, where the species range through sand sedge, golden dock, fritillaries, orchids, meadow saffron, moonwort fern, lady's mantle and spiny restharrow.

Forest and woodland

Scarcely anything remains of the ancient Suffolk wildwood; even the dense shadowy 'thicks' of broad oaks and hollies, undisturbed for centuries, rarely date back that far. Following earlier clearance, Suffolk at Domesday was less wooded than many other counties. Today's native woodlands are diverse and well stocked with deer. Acidic soils encourage alder, hazel, holly, small-leafed lime and some birch, also honeysuckle, primrose, bluebell and wood anemone. More alkaline soils support ash, elm, field maple, dogwood, spindle and guelder-rose. On richer clays may be found dog's mercury, oxlip and herb-paris.

Timber for building and shipbuilding and oak bark for the leather industry were extracted from managed woodland. Surrounding underwood was cut cyclically to promote new growth, by coppicing or pollarding. Cuttings from hornbeam, ash and hazel were ideal for tool handles, rustic poles, hurdles, wattles and thatch fixings.

Softwood forests are much more recent, the majority having been planted since the 1920s to supply local industry. They provide good woodland walking through the avenues or rides used for extracting timber. In the drier areas, with soils of low fertility, Corsican pine grows well but it is vulnerable to gales like that of October 1987, when Suffolk lost over a million trees in a few hours.

All the places described in this chapter are understood at the time of writing to be open to the public unless specifically mentioned otherwise. Visitors should follow the Country Code.

The following organisations are responsible for sites described in this chapter, and further information may be obtained from them.

English Nature, Norman Tower, 1-2 Crown Street, Bury St Edmunds IP33 1QX. Telephone: 01284 762218.

Royal Society for the Protection of Birds, Stalham House, 65 Thorpe Road, Norwich, Norfolk NR1 1UD. Telephone: 01603 661662.

Suffolk County Council, St Edmund House, County Hall, Ipswich IP4 1LZ. Telephone: 01473 230000.

Suffolk Wildlife Trust, Brooke House, The Green, Ashbocking, Ipswich IP6 9JY. Telephone: 01473 890089.

Angles Way (OS 134, 144).

Angles Way is a 77 mile (124 km) path leading through Norfolk and Suffolk from Great Yarmouth to Knettishall Heath Country Park in Breckland, linking the Icknield Way, Bigod Way, Waveney Way and Waveney Trails. It crosses Beccles Marshes and passes Hopton, Hoxne, Mendham, Bungay and Beccles – once the area of the hemp industry. A leaflet is available from Suffolk County Council.

Arger Fen, Bures (OS 155: TL 930355). 5 miles (8 km) south-west of Sudbury. Suffolk County Council.

Set amongst rolling countryside, paths lead through undulating bluebell woods with splendid wild cherry trees (leaflet available from the county council). Just to the north is Spouses Grove (Suffolk Wildlife Trust), an area of ancient woodland sheltering nightingales, bluebells and yellow-necked mice.

Benacre National Nature Reserve (OS 156: TM 520820). 4¼ miles (7 km) south of Lowestoft.

This reserve includes the broads of Benacre, Covehithe and Easton, which are set in a varied landscape ranging through beach, dunes, woodland, reedbeds and hay meadow. Please keep to the public footpath.

Bigod Way (OS 134, 156).

This 10 mile (16 km) walk orbiting Beccles crosses the Waveney and passes Earsham church and Mettingham Castle. It includes Constitution Stroll, Scotchman's Lane, Bath Hills Walk and Rabbitskin Run.

Blaxhall Common (OS 156: TM 382565). Straddles B1069 just south-west of Snape. Suffolk Wildlife Trust.

This area of ancient common heath and grazing land is now bordered by pine and birch woods. Man's contributions include an iron age burial mound and trenches dug to stop German gliders landing in the Second World War.

Bonny Wood and Priestley Wood (OS 155: TM 076520 and 080530). 1¾ miles (3 km) south of Needham Market. Suffolk Wildlife Trust.

Both reserves were part of the ancient Barking woods compulsorily purchased in 1561 by Queen Elizabeth I from the Bishop of Ely. There is small-leafed lime, much coppiced, plus wild pear, ash and maple which shade orchids, garlic and helleborine. A leaflet is available from the Trust. Bonny Wood is a Site of Special Scientific Interest.

Boyton Marshes (OS 169: TM 390470). Just south-east of Boyton. Access only from public footpaths. Suffolk Wildlife Trust.

This is a remote coastal saltmarsh with drainage ditches, overlooking Havergate Island. Abundant birdlife includes warblers, ducks and swans.

Bradfield Woods (OS 155: TL 935581). 6 miles (9 km) south-east of Bury St Edmunds. Suffolk Wildlife Trust. Site of Special Scientific Interest.

Mostly ancient woodland, trees here have been coppiced since medieval times when they were owned by Bury Abbey: Monks' Park remains. Thus there are large oaks and secondary woodland with a clearing from the old deer park. The visitor centre gives access to rides full of wildlife and a great diversity of plants, probably unchanged for centuries. A leaflet is available from the Trust.

Brandon Country Park, Brandon (OS 144: TL 788854). Telephone: 01842 810185. Just south of Brandon, off B1106. Suffolk County Council.

The visitor centre and walled garden lead to forest walks, tree trails and a wayfaring course past the lake and mausoleum. (The house itself is closed to the public.) There are feral golden pheasants, jays, long-tailed tits, squirrels, deer and adders. A leaflet is available from the county council.

Bromeswell Green and Wilford Bridge (OS 156: TM 296504). Just north-east of Woodbridge. Suffolk Wildlife Trust.

Grassland, woodland, reedbeds and marsh border a nature trail near the river Deben. Nightingales, kingfishers and warblers thrive on this site which in 1803 supported a Napoleonic war camp.

Bulls Wood (OS 155: TL 917547). 1¼ miles (2 km) east of Cockfield (between Bury St Edmunds and Lavenham). Suffolk Wildlife Trust. Site of Special Scientific Interest.

This ancient coppiced woodland is mainly hazel and ash, with flowers such as oxlip, spurge-laurel, early purple orchid and Oregon grape.

Camps Heath and Oulton Marshes (OS 134: TM 509941). 1¼ miles (2 km) north-west of Lowestoft. Suffolk Wildlife Trust. Site of Special Scientific Interest.

This is an area of dyked herb-rich grazing marsh which shelters bog pimpernel and marsh cinquefoil. Amongst the reeds, alder and willow are woodcock, siskins and warblers.

Carlton Marshes, Carlton Colville (OS 134: TM 508920). Telephone: 01502 564250. 1¼ miles (2 km) west of Lowestoft at the tip of Oulton Broad. Suffolk Wildlife Trust. Site of Special Scientific Interest.

Amongst dyked grazing marsh, fen and old peat diggings off the Waveney Way, the visitor centre shows a wetland display of local species which include cowbane, frogbit, marsh pea, water-soldier and abundant dragonflies.

Cavenham Heath National Nature Reserve (OS 155: TL 750725). 3 miles (5 km) east of Mildenhall. English Nature. Public access only to area south of Tuddenham-Icklingham track (car park at Temple Bridge).

This mixed habitat lies partly by the river Lark, including the heather, gorse, bracken and scrub of acid heathland, as well as woodland, fen and willow carr. This supports such flowers as dark mullein and mignonette and birds including gadwall, pipits and whinchat.

Clare Country Park, Clare (OS 155: TL 768451). Telephone: 01787 277491. Suffolk County Council.

A 3½ mile (6 km) circular walk tours the earthworks and old moats of the Norman castle, a millstream and butterfly garden. The park office is Clare's former railway station. A leaflet is available from Suffolk County Council.

Combs Wood (OS 155: TM 053568). Half a mile (1 km) south of Stowmarket, off B1113.

The visitor centre at Brandon Country Park on the edge of Breckland.

Suffolk Wildlife Trust. Site of Special Scientific Interest.

The ancient coppiced woodland here rises over a chalky hilltop; below the hornbeam are damp flowery woodland rides.

Cornard Mere (OS 155: TL 887388). Just south of Sudbury, off B1508. Suffolk Wildlife Trust. Site of Special Scientific Interest.

This is an area of marshland and open water in the Stour valley with a reputation for bogbean, tufted sedge and barn owls.

Darsham Marshes (OS 156: TM 420691). 1¼ miles (2 km) north-east of Yoxford. Suffolk Wildlife Trust.

In this part of the Minsmere valley the water level is controlled by sluices, resulting in fen, extensive grazing marsh and acid grassy heathland. There are birds of prey, frogs and toads. A leaflet is available from the Trust.

Dunwich Heath and Dunwich Common (OS 156: TM 476685). Telephone: 01728 73505. 1¼ miles (2 km) south of Dunwich. National Trust.

The visitor centre occupies old coastguard cottages on the steep sandy cliff, providing excellent views over the sea and to Minsmere. Inland, a rolling heathland of heather, bracken, gorse, broom and willowherb unfurls, with purple moor-grass in damper areas and glimpses of yellowhammers and linnets.

Fen Alder Carr, Creeting St Peter (OS 155: TM 089569). 1¼ miles (2 km) north of Needham Market. Suffolk County Council.

This wetland nature reserve, with a boardwalk path over the wet bog, provides a warm humid microclimate in summer. Marsh marigolds, ramsons and lush vegetation shelter water voles and frogs. The alder trees were originally planted to supply raw materials for the gunpowder factory at Stowmarket.

Foxburrow Wood, Yarmouth Road, Lowestoft (OS 134: TM 535956). Suffolk Wildlife Trust.

Many fine trees can be found amongst broadleaf woodland and ancient hazel and hornbeam coppices, around ponds and streams. There are spring bluebells and anemones.

Framlingham Mere, Framlingham (OS 156: TM 283636). Beside the castle. Suffolk Wildlife Trust.

This circular walk through water-meadows around the shallow mere gives good views of the castle and of wading birds. Sedges flourish in the fen, which was dug out around 1190.

Freston Woods, Shotley Peninsula (OS 169: TM 172397). 1³/4 miles (3 km) south of Ipswich off B1456.

A good view of the Orwell Bridge can be obtained from this ancient woodland, which includes very old sweet-chestnut. Not far away, Spring Wood at Wherstead (OS 169: TM 144419; Suffolk Wildlife Trust) comprises further ancient woodland with hornbeams and small-leafed limes. A leaflet is available from the county council.

Gipping Valley River Path (OS 155, 169).

This path extends for 17 miles (27 km) from Ipswich Wet Dock to Stowmarket along the towpath of the Ipswich-Stowmarket Navigation via Darmsden, Badley and Bramford. Bramford Meadows is an area of ditched wet woodland managed by Gipping Valley Project. There are substantial watermills en route at Sproughton, Baylham and Bosmere, and alternative footpaths through Shrubland Park. A leaflet is available from the county council.

Groton Wood (OS 155: TL 976428). 3 miles (5 km) west of Hadleigh. Suffolk Wildlife Trust. Site of Special Scientific Interest.

This nature trail passes ponds, ditches and flowery glades with sweet woodruff and herb-paris, whose poisonous berries were once used against witchcraft. There are remains of ancient broadleaf woodland, mostly cleared and replanted at the Reformation. At that time the wood passed from Bury Abbey to the Winthrop family of Groton, one of whose descendants, sailing with a charter from Charles I, became first governor of Massachusetts. Here is the largest stand in Suffolk of slow-growing small-leafed lime or pry, often used for intricate woodcarving in churches. A leaflet is available from the Trust.

The Haven, Thorpeness (OS 156: TM 470587). Suffolk Wildlife Trust.

This shingle beach and marshland reserve shelters plants such as sea pea, sand catchfly and bur medick and attracts migrant birds. To the west, where the habitat includes reedbeds and rough grassland, this reserve borders North Warren (page 67).

Havergate Island National Nature Reserve (OS 169: TM 420480). 1¹/4 miles (2 km) south of Orford. Royal Society for the Protection of Birds.

This reserve may be visited from April to August, by boat from Orford quay. Once a smugglers' bleak refuge, regularly flooded, the island was embanked to graze cattle. Now its shallow brackish lagoons and shingly saltmarsh provide breeding grounds for many birds including terns and avocets, reintroduced in 1947.

Hazelwood Marshes (OS 156: TM 435575). 1³/4 miles (3 km) west of Aldeburgh off A1094. Suffolk Wildlife Trust. Site of Special Scientific Interest.

This area of coastal grazing marsh, tidal mudflats and reedbeds attracts wading and migrant birds. It is accessible from the Sailors' Path, an old smuggling trail linking Aldeburgh and Snape. (There is no access to the river wall.)

Henham Walks, Henham Park (OS 156: TM 454775). Telephone: 01502 78424. 3 miles (5 km) west of Southwold.

A variety of walks lead from Wangford Lodge over the estate of the Australian Earl and Countess of Stradbroke.

Hollesley Heath (OS 169: TM 347466). 1¹/4 miles (2 km) north of Hollesley. Suffolk Wildlife Trust. Site of Special Scientific Interest.

This Sandlings area combines heathland with Scots pines and birch woodland sheltering deer, adders and bats. It is still recovering from the effects of the 1987 hurricane.

Hopton Fen, Hopton (OS 144: TL 990800). 6¹/4 miles (10 km) north-east of Ixworth. Suffolk Wildlife Trust. Site of Special

Scientific Interest.

This secluded and moist valley fen reserve supports chalk-loving flora and fenland birds. Keep away from the fen peat, which can be dangerous.

Icknield Way (OS 144, 154, 155).

The Icknield Way links the Ridgeway in Buckinghamshire to Peddars Way at Knettishall Heath. It follows a neolithic route three thousand years old which connected south central England to the Norfolk coast, bypassing fen and forest along a chalky ridge. Medieval travellers on this route were protected by the King's Peace – it was one of the four great roads of England noted under Edward the Confessor, used for droving cattle, for transporting salt, and as a pilgrimage route to Walsingham. The 28 miles (45 km) in Suffolk shadowing the original route, are full of archaeological interest and pass through the villages of Dalham, Herringswell, Icklingham and Euston. A leaflet is available from the county council describing routes for walkers and horse-riders.

Iken Cliff (OS 156: TM 398561). 1^1/4 miles (2 km) south-east of Snape. Suffolk County Council. Site of Special Scientific Interest.

A boardwalk path links this area to Snape Concert Hall and its famous estuarine reedbed views. To the east, visible from Iken church, the Alde mudflats are rich in wading birds, especially during winter.

Knettishall Heath Country Park (OS 144: TL 956806). Telephone: 01953 818265. 6^1/4 miles (10 km) north of Ixworth. Suffolk County Council. Site of Special Scientific Interest.

This park marks the intersection point of Peddars Way, Angles Way and the Icknield Way. Much of it is Breckland heath with rabbit warrens, but there is also a frontage on to the Little Ouse river, mixed woodland and grassland supporting wavy hair grass, heath bedstraw, tormentil, harebell and, in more chalky areas, dropwort and salad burnet. A leaflet is available from the county council.

Lackford Wildfowl Reserve (OS 144, 155: TL 803708). 4^1/4 miles (7 km) north-west of

Bury St Edmunds, off A1101. Suffolk Wildlife Trust. Site of Special Scientific Interest.

These worked-out gravel pits in the Lark valley are equipped with hides to observe wildfowl such as goosander, kingfisher, osprey and black tern. There is a also wide range of marshland flowers. A leaflet is available on site.

Ladygate Wood (OS 154: TL 654441). 1^1/4 miles (2 km) south-west of Haverhill. Suffolk Wildlife Trust.

This is a small area of ancient woodland with associated ground cover of wood avens, sanicle and oxlip.

Lakenheath Poors Fen and Pashford Poors Fen (OS 143: TL 702827). The former is 1^1/4 miles (2 km) west of Lakenheath; the latter is 1^1/4 miles (2 km) east of Lakenheath. Suffolk Wildlife Trust.

These areas of wet and dry sandy fen encourage many marsh plants and willows, great fen-sedge, purple small-reed and bog myrtle. There are also snipe, songbirds and dragonflies.

Landguard Point (OS 169: TM 285315). A promontory south of Felixstowe. Suffolk Wildlife Trust and Suffolk County Council. Site of Special Scientific Interest.

Below Landguard Fort the pebble beach undulates into a spit which extends from the river Orwell into the North Sea. Its diverse habitat, affected by strong winter winds and hot summers, encourages sea kale on the beach, then short turf with vetch and stinking goosefoot. Inland there is scrub, tamarisk, brambles and woodland. Seabirds and migrant birds are ringed at the bird observatory (telephone: 01394 673782 – public access on open days) and there are plentiful butterflies.

Lark Valley Path (OS 143, 144, 155).

This is a 13 mile (21 km) Breckland walk from Mildenhall to Bury St Edmunds via Icklingham, Flempton and Hengrave. The path loosely follows the river Lark through an area well settled in neolithic times, passing the King's Forest, West Stow Country Park and Lackford Wildfowl Reserve.

Leathes Ham (OS 134: TM 533935). Beside Normanston Park, Lowestoft. Suffolk Wildlife Trust.

This is an urban wildfowl sanctuary located between dockland and a railway. It offers open water, reedbeds and woodland for newts, bats and a wide variety of birds.

Market Weston Fen (OS 144: TL 981789). 5 miles (8 km) north of Walsham le Willows. Suffolk Wildlife Trust. Site of Special Scientific Interest.

An interesting valley fen, with great fensedge which is still cut for thatching, this environmentally rich area includes ponds, dry heath and grassland, sedge beds and plants such as betony.

Martin's Meadow, Monewden (OS 156: TM 227573). 3³/4 miles (6 km) south-west of Framlingham. Suffolk Wildlife Trust.

These three traditional flower-rich hay meadows, with orchards and old hedges, contain a range of grassland species and wild flowers. Please keep to the paths.

Mickfield Meadow, Stonham Aspal (OS 156: TM 143633). 6 miles (9 km) east of Stowmarket, off A1120. Suffolk Wildlife Trust. Site of Special Scientific Interest.

This wetland meadow is full of herbs and flowers such as fritillaries, ragged robin and wild angelica. Please keep to the paths.

Mid Suffolk Footpath (OS 155, 156).

This route links Hoxne and Stowmarket (and thereby the rivers Dove and Gipping) across 20 miles (32 km) of river valleys and farmland, crossing the 'Middy' Railway Footpath and pausing at the wildlife reserve of The Pennings. En route are Eye, Thorndon and Mendlesham.

Minsmere Nature Reserve, Westleton, Saxmundham IP17 3BY (OS 156: TM 452680). Telephone: 01728 648281. 3 miles (5 km) north of Leiston. Royal Society for the Protection of Birds.
Open daily, except Tuesdays.

This is an important bird reserve with a visitor centre, nature trails and observation hides. Wildlife includes avocet, marsh harrier, water rail, waders and migrants; there are also water voles, red deer, muntjac and silver-studded blue butterflies. Many birds breed here and over a hundred different species have been recorded in a single day. They are attracted to the range of different habitats: reedbeds, dunes, shore, heathland and woods. There is also the man-made Scrape, an area of shallow lagoons rich in shrimp.

Nacton Meadows, Nacton (OS 169: TM 232400). 3³/4 miles (6 km) south-east of Ipswich. Suffolk Wildlife Trust. Site of Special Scientific Interest.

These are picturesque meadows in the Orwell valley in which grow rushes, orchids and other wild flowers. Please keep to the path.

Newbourne Springs, Newbourne (OS 169: TM 271433). 3³/4 miles (6 km) south of Woodbridge. Anglian Water and Suffolk Wildlife Trust. Site of Special Scientific Interest.

Swamp alder carr in the valley bottom rises to reedbeds, acid grassland and dry woodland. From 1930 to 1980 these ponds, springs and streams provided a local water supply, now superseded by Alton Reservoir. The visitor centre is not far from an old coprolite pit. A leaflet is available from the Trust.

Norman Gwatkin (OS 156: TM 463765). 2¹/2 miles (4 km) west of Southwold. Suffolk Wildlife Trust.

Named after Sir Norman Gwatkin, this is a marsh and fenland area with osier beds. Alder carr and crack, grey and white willows provide cover for sedges, fungi, rushes, frogs, toads, grass snakes and wading birds.

North Cove (OS 134: TM 471906). 3 miles (5 km) east of Beccles. Suffolk Wildlife Trust. Site of Special Scientific Interest.

This mixture of mature woodland and marsh, with pools and dykes, lies beside the river Waveney. Woodpeckers, nightingales and owls may be seen.

Northfield Wood, Onehouse (OS 155: TM 023600). 1¹/4 miles (2 km) north-west of

Stowmarket. Woodland Trust.

Broadleaf trees and remnants of ancient woodland thrive alongside conifer plantations. The wide rides are well stocked with flowers such as anemones.

North Warren (OS 156: TM 452595). 1³/4 miles (3 km) north of Aldeburgh off B1122. Royal Society for the Protection of Birds.

This Sandlings area of heath, reedbed, acid grassland and coastal grazing marsh supports a variety of dragonflies, moths and butterflies such as the grayling, clouded yellow and gate-keeper. The birds include bitterns, bearded tits and thousands of waders and wintering wildfowl

Orford Ness National Nature Reserve (OS 169. TM 450490). 1¹/4 miles (2 km) east of Orford. National Trust. (Access by ferry only, see page 122.)

This remarkable and remote shingle spit has been extending south for centuries, keeping the Alde and Ore river from the North Sea; it now shelters Orford, Havergate Island, Boyton Marshes and the Butley River. Such a specialised habitat has fostered lichens and mosses as well as typical salt-loving plants. It is an important landfall for migratory birds and accommodates great colonies of gulls.

Peddars Way

This follows the route of the Roman road which by AD 61 led from the military garrison at Colchester to the Wash via Stowlangtoft, Knettishall and Woolpit. It is a National Trail designated by the Countryside Commission.

Redgrave and Lopham Fens National Nature Reserve (OS 144: TM 046797). 5 miles (8 km) west of Diss, off B1113. Suffolk Wildlife Trust. Site of Special Scientific Interest.

This area of wetland divides Suffolk and Norfolk, offering nature trails past river valleys, bogs, pools and ditches growing shoulder-high reeds and sedges – the result of peat digging. Amongst the mosses, cotton grass, grass of Parnassus and common butterwort is the home of the great raft spider, the biggest spider in Britain, discovered in 1956. A leaf-

let is available from the Trust.

Rendlesham Forest (OS 156, 169: TM 340500). 4¹/4 miles (7 km) east of Woodbridge on B1084.

Together with Tunstall and Dunwich Forest this forms the Aldewood Forest, which, prior to coniferous planting by the Forestry Commission in the 1920s, was open heathland used for grazing sheep. See Tang Valley Trail, page 68.

Reydon Wood (OS 156: TM 479787). 3³/4 miles (6 km) north-west of Southwold. Suffolk Wildlife Trust.

This ancient coppiced woodland includes rides, an old green lane and a ditch against deer. Conifers planted in the 1960s are now being removed to replant native hardwoods, which are also regenerating from huge stumps. The nature trail winds through blue-bells, orchids, moschatel and yellow arch-angel. A leaflet is available from the Trust.

St Cross Farm Walks (OS 156: TM 307833). 4¹/4 miles (7 km) south-west of Bungay.

The walks lead around St Cross South Elmham through an historic landscape, now remote, which includes the remains of the Minster and a former bishop's palace. British White cattle may be seen grazing in former parkland.

St Edmund Way (OS 144, 155, 169).

This unofficial 88 mile (142 km) walk (not signposted) leads from Manningtree to Brandon, along the river Stour to Long Melford, then north through Lavenham, Bury St Edmunds and West Stow.

Simpson's Saltings, Hollesley (OS 169: TM 383453). 6¹/4 miles (10 km) south-east of Woodbridge. Suffolk Wildlife Trust. Site of Special Scientific Interest.

Named after a Suffolk botanist, this saltmarsh reserve is characterised by plants like sea kale, sea pea and sea heath. Birds nest in the wartime concrete pillboxes.

Stanton Rides, Stanton (OS 144: TL 965735).

The rides extend over some 18 miles (29

km) of waymarked rights of way and minor roads leading from the countryside around Stanton north to Hopton.

Staverton Thicks, Butley (OS 156: TM 360505). 3³/₄ miles (6 km) west of Orford.

Huge specimens of medieval pollarded oaks and hollies, with the occasional rhododendron, occupy land enclosed by an earth dyke for a deer park in the thirteenth century. The local monks entertained the queen of France here for a picnic in 1528.

Stour Valley Path (OS 154, 155, 169).

This is a 60 mile (97 km) walk from Newmarket to Manningtree, passing through Flatford and Dedham Vale. It interlinks with other walks, for example at Wissington, and is a Countryside Commission designated Regional Route.

Suffolk Heritage Coast Path (or Suffolk Coast and Heaths Path) (OS 134, 156, 169).

This extends 50 miles (80 km) from Lowestoft to Bawdsey and on to Felixstowe, ferry permitting. It hugs the coast, crossing occasional woods and heathland, past Thorpeness, Dunwich and Covehithe. Points of interest include Burrow Hill, Snape Maltings, shingle beaches, sandy cliffs and several martello towers. An additional ferry across Butley Creek gives access to Orford. A leaflet is available from the county council.

Sutton Heath and Common (OS 169: TM 335472). 3 miles (5 km) south-east of Woodbridge on B1083.

This is a nature trail through a protected area of the Sandlings, adjacent to broadleaf and coniferous woodland. It includes a medieval rabbit warren.

Tang Valley Trail (OS 169: TM 355484). Telephone: 01394 450164. 6 miles (9 km) east of Woodbridge, off B1084 by the Forest Enterprise District Office, Rendlesham Forest, Woodbridge.

This Forestry Commission trail explores an area of Rendlesham Forest devastated by the 1987 October gale. It has now been replanted, mixing broadleaf trees around the Corsican pine cash crop. Kingfishers frequent ponds beside the river. A leaflet is available from the above office.

Thelnetham Fen (OS 144: TM 016786). 6³/₄ miles (11 km) west of Diss. Suffolk Wildlife Trust. Site of Special Scientific Interest.

The Middle Fen and Old Fen (bordering the Little Ouse river) are at risk from drying out, but the wetter areas still support plants like black bogrush and marsh lousewort.

Thetford Forest (OS 144). Telephone: 01842 815434. Between Brandon and Bury St Edmunds. Including the King's Forest, named after George V.
Visitor centres open Easter to September.

This is Britain's largest lowland Scots and Corsican pine forest. Commercial softwood is produced here. The felled and recently re-

An ancient oak amid holly trees in Staverton Thicks.

planted areas attract woodlarks and nightjars, the mature pines crossbills. There are deer and squirrels. Thetford Forest Park includes Forest Drive and a network of paths, cycle trails and bridleways with visitor centres at Lynford Stag, the Arboretum, High Lodge and Forest Lodge (just north of West Stow).

Thornham Walks, Thornham Magna (OS 155: TM 105723). Telephone: 01379 788153. 1¼ miles (2 km) south of Mellis. *Open daily except for some Wednesdays and Saturdays.*

Footpaths over farmland, woodland, parkland and wet meadowland are linked with a field study centre which has a walled garden, scent garden and butterfly walk.

Toby's Walks, Blythburgh (OS 156: TM 447743). 2½ miles (4 km) west of Walberswick.

Tobias Gill, a black drummer in a dragoon regiment, was executed in 1750 on a false charge of murder; his ghost, and those of four headless horses, are said to haunt Blythburgh Heath, the site of these pleasant walks.

Trimley Marshes (OS 169: TM 278358). 1¼ miles (2 km) west of Felixstowe. Suffolk Wildlife Trust.

This reserve was formed when Felixstowe Dock expanded. Wet grazing marsh, reedbeds and lagoons have been created from former farmland and the resulting wildfowl, waders and hares can be watched from the visitor centre and hides.

Walberswick National Nature Reserve (OS 156: TM 460730). Just south of Walberswick. English Nature.

This is probably the most diverse reserve in Suffolk, encompassing a huge area of reedbeds, estuarine mudflats, shoreline, grazing marshes, sandy heathland and mixed woodland. Many varieties of birds and unusual insects may be seen. Access is by 20 miles (32 km) of public footpath only.

Wangford Warren (OS 143: TL 756842). 3 miles (5 km) south-west of Brandon off A1065. Suffolk Wildlife Trust. Site of Special Scientific Interest.

Access may be restricted in spring and summer when birds are breeding. This is the largest active sand-dune system in the area, once managed for rabbit production. Sand movement brings diverse vegetation including lichens, mosses and grey hair-grass.

Westleton Heath National Nature Reserve (OS 156: TM 450690). The reserve straddles the road between Westleton and Dunwich, public access is only to the north and along rights of way. English Nature.

This part of the Sandlings is characterised by heather heath with some mixed woodland.

West Stow Country Park (OS 144, 155: TL 801715). Telephone: 01284 728718. 4¼ miles (7 km) north-west of Bury St Edmunds. St Edmundsbury Borough Council.

This nature reserve encompasses grassland, woodland and a lake covering former gravel workings.

Winks Meadow, Metfield (OS 156: TM 303798). 5 miles (8 km) north of Laxfield. Suffolk Wildlife Trust. Site of Special Scientific Interest.

This is a typical ancient meadow growing many wild flowers including orchids.

Wolves Wood, Aldham (OS 155: TM 054436). 1¾ miles (3 km) east of Hadleigh, off A1071. Royal Society for the Protection of Birds.

This reserve comprises mixed woodland – oak, ash, hornbeam, hazel and grey willow. Local boulder clay has produced a high water table; mosses, ferns, aspen and sallow flourish in the wetter areas, which include ponds. Hides, an information hut and waymarked paths may assist in seeing up to fifty species of breeding birds.

Wortham Ling (OS 144: TM 091797). 2½ miles (4 km) north-west of Mellis. Suffolk Wildlife Trust. Site of Special Scientific Interest.

Beside the river Waveney, this common land is mostly heath with acid, chalk and neutral grassland, encouraging butterflies. It merges into gorse scrub and woodland.

4
Places of archaeological interest

Neolithic Suffolk (4200-2200 BC) was well populated by people who cleared woodland, farmed, raised livestock and built earthwork enclosures and burial mounds, although none of the latter are on display in the county.

Later, bronze age people grew cereals, processed flax, used flint tools, made pottery and are best remembered for their barrows, up to 100 feet (30 metres) in diameter and 8 feet (2.4 metres) high. Fewer than a hundred small examples survive in Breckland and the Sandlings; examples can be seen in Knettishall Heath Country Park at Hut Hill.

Life became more aggressive during the iron age (800 BC to AD 43) and hillforts were built. It is possible that Erbury (now Clare Camp), which occupies a grassy 7 acre (2.8 hectare) space within a double bank and ditch, belongs to this period. Prestige metalworking and imported wines were enjoyed. Six decorated gold and silver collars from 1 BC were found at Ipswich in 1968 and have been described as one of the richest iron age hoards in England.

At this time Suffolk was populated by the Iceni in the north and the Trinovantes in the south, whose frontier took roughly the route of today's A14. In their turn, these tribes were subjugated by the Romans with formidable military roads which included Pye Street and Peddars Way linking, for example, *Ad Ansam* (Stratford St Mary), *Sitomagus* (location uncertain) and *Combretonium* (Coddenham), a fortified ford of the river Gipping which the Romans elevated to a posting station, camp and maybe an imperial shrine. It is now an attractive village at OS 156: TM 134543.

Roman Suffolk revolved around markets, distribution centres and pottery kilns. By the fourth century some individuals had become rich enough to build villas with tiled floors, painted walls and hypocausts as at Whitton (the mosaic is in Ipswich Museum). There

were also forts, as at Pakenham, where a 7 acre (2.8 hectare) enclosure with triple ditches controlled a river crossing. Along the coast, a chain of military bases called the Saxon Shore forts was raised to repulse seaborne raiders, but little survives: Walton Castle, near Felixstowe, is under the sea and substantial Burgh Castle is now in Norfolk. These defences were breached in AD 367 and the forts abandoned around AD 407 when the Romans left, many burying their treasures.

In 1938 the Mildenhall treasure, a collection of embossed silver dishes and goblets decorated with pagan and Christian symbols, was unearthed at Mildenhall and is now in the British Museum. Other discoveries have included the Eye hoard, the Icklingham bronzes and the Thetford treasure. The last, uncovered in 1979, comprises eighty-three objects, including silver spoons and gold chains. In 1990 excavations at Boss Hall, Ipswich, yielded jewels, brooches and beads. These are all overshadowed by the Hoxne treasure, discovered in 1992 and now in the British Museum. This great Roman hoard of two hundred valuables includes a gold, pearl and amethyst body chain, a solid silver prancing tigress and many spoons and bracelets, some inscribed 'Aurelius Ursicinus'. There were also 14,870 coins struck in mints from Trier to Antioch.

As the Roman Empire collapsed, Suffolk entered a dark age: Saxon warlords and opportunists in long boats from what is now Germany and Denmark came looking for farmland; rivers like the Stour provided ideal access inland. Such incursions precipitated many battles and Saxon settlements were established, often moated with wooden palisades to contain cattle. At West Stow a Saxon village has been reconstructed – a cluster of timbered houses with walls of wattle and daub, planked floors and sedge roofs (page 71).

The Wuffing tribes arrived from Sweden early in the sixth century, sailing up the Deben to settle around Woodbridge, and building a palace near Rendlesham. They were powerful and under their leader Raedwald (*c*.599-625) the first Anglo-Saxon kingdom of East Anglia was established. Raedwald's background was pagan, worshipping Woden, but he was baptised and pragmatically kept altars both to the old and the new gods. Thus it was a Christian Raedwald who became 'Bretwalda' or High King, ruling for nine years over the seven kingdoms which would eventually become England; he was buried in the royal cemetery at Sutton Hoo.

The new religion was assisted from Rome. Thus came men like St Felix, a Burgundian monk who became the first Bishop of Dunwich in AD 626. Schools and monasteries followed and over fifty wooden churches were dedicated before 900, suggesting some political stability despite continuing incursions from abroad. Perhaps it was to consolidate this kingdom that a variety of earthworks, all orientated north-west/southeast, were strengthened at this time, such as Black Ditches (OS 155: TL 766720) and maybe even the curious, unexplained Grundles (OS 155: TL 973724 and TM 015745).

These inadequate defences were crossed in AD 654 in one of many Mercian invasions. A later foray, in 792, resulted in Offa, king of Mercia, beheading St Ethelbert, then king of East Anglia. Further intruders came from Wessex and Denmark, led by men like Ivan the Boneless, whose great heathen army landed *c*.859 to ravage the farms and monasteries. Resistance was focused in Christian King Edmund, whom the Danes captured and executed in 869.

Danelaw began in AD 880, ruling England east of Watling Street, attracting further Scandinavians, who named land after themselves, as at Herringfleet or Blundeston. Allied incursions continued: in 991, ninety-three boatloads of Norsemen overran Ipswich and in 1010 Bury St Edmunds was sacked by Thorkell the Tall and King Swein Forkbeard, whose successor, Canute, defeated the king of Wessex in 1016 to become king of England. King Canute remembered his East Anglian roots, generously contributing to Bury and its abbey.

Anglo-Saxon Village, Icklingham Road, West Stow, Bury St Edmunds IP28 6EZ (OS 144, 155: TL 801714). Telephone: 01284 728718. 6 miles (9 km) north-west of Bury St Edmunds, off A1101 (within West Stow Country Park, see page 69).
Open daily.

This site was settled in mesolithic, iron age and Roman times and the Saxons occupied it from AD 420 to 650, leaving sufficient evidence to allow a Saxon reconstruction, which took place in 1965-72, producing a group of thatched timber houses and halls. Further research now makes possible demonstrations based on Anglo-Saxon life, illustrating its crafts, clothing and food.

Sutton Hoo, Sutton, Woodbridge IP12 3DJ (OS 169: TM 288488). 1¼ miles (2 km) east of Woodbridge, off B1083.
Open weekend afternoons from April to September.

A series of barrows rises from a plateau overlooking the river Deben; visitors see little beyond these and a simple Anglo-Saxon display. The largest barrow was opened in 1939 to reveal, Beowulf-like, the outline of a longboat used for ritual burial, almost certainly of Raedwald. It was clinker-built, 89 feet (27 metres) long by 14 feet (4.5 metres) across, well used but without a sail. There was no evidence of a body, despite provisions for an afterlife including an iron lamp, pottery bottle, mail shirt and axe hammer. There were treasures: a decorated iron helmet, a sword with gold and cloisonné fittings and a pattern-welded blade, a shield with elaborate iron boss. All are now in the British Museum. Ongoing excavations have revealed earlier remains, and, from another era, contorted bodies suggesting sacrifice or execution. Mediterranean silverware was also found at Sutton Hoo.

5
Castles and monastic ruins

In 1086 the Domesday survey revealed Suffolk to have one of the densest populations in England; most of today's major towns and villages were already in existence.

William the Conqueror rewarded his friends with land and manors, creating in Suffolk three powerful Norman magnates. Thus, for assistance at the battle of Hastings, Roger Bigod acquired 117 manors and his ambitious family administered them from castles at Ipswich, Felixstowe, Thetford and Norwich. Richard de Clare was William's Chief Justice; he helped stifle a revolt in 1076 and gained ninety-five lordships. William Malet, based at Eye, received 221 holdings; he was killed fighting Hereward the Wake. His son founded Eye Priory but in 1110 plotted against the king, and as a result lost the family's castle at Eye.

Early castles were timber buildings on earth mounds above wet ditches. Some earthworks survive, as at Denham Castle (OS 155: TL 747629; footpath access only) and Haughley Castle, built around 1100 on a motte 80 feet (24 metres) high – its moat is the village pond.

Timber fortifications were superseded by stone castles. By 1165 the powerful Bigod family effectively ruled Suffolk, unchallenged until Henry II took a stand, completing Orford Castle in 1173. Royal troops took the rebel Bigod power bases: Framlingham was destroyed but at Bungay the king was bought off. In due course the Bigod family rebuilt both castles!

In 1338, during the Hundred Years War, Edward III assembled a fleet of forty ships near Felixstowe to fight the French. The same estuaries which had brought foreign invaders into Suffolk now sheltered the English navy. Suffolk's ports began to prosper from foreign trade and fishing.

Further inland, towns flourished, markets were licensed, churches raised and farming expanded. Political stability lessened the need for castles and generous timber-framed buildings were constructed.

After the Norman conquest the growing religious orders became wealthy landowners, controlling towns and countryside, enabling the construction in masonry of abbeys and priories. They levied rents and taxes, for example on beer, sometimes provoking riots, such as in 1327 when the abbey of St Edmundsbury was sacked and burnt.

In 1528 Cardinal Wolsey (page 125) secured a papal bull to shut forty 'religious houses', including priories at Snape and Ipswich, to raise funds for his Cardinal College of St Mary in Ipswich. Henry VIII took up this idea nationally, suppressing six hundred 'religious houses' for his own funds, and in 1534 he replaced the Pope as head of the English church. Two years later Henry VIII's 'Act for the Dissolution of the Lesser Monasteries' closed, amongst others, Sibton Abbey, Leiston Abbey, Butley Priory, Clare Priory and Eye Monastery. Many of these buildings were ruined, becoming quarries or sites for new buildings like Christchurch Mansion. Powerful Bury St Edmunds Abbey held out until 1539, then it went too. Religious assets were surrendered to the Crown, which sold them, buying off the abbots and priors. At Dunwich, Greyfriars was privatised and let out at an annual rent of 7s 6d; its buildings were mostly razed. There followed further upheaval with the dissolution of chantries and guilds, effectively closing the guildhalls.

From 1651 to 1674 three fishery wars were fought against the Dutch, the biggest battle being off Sole Bay, Southwold, in May 1672, involving nearly three hundred ships; each side claimed victory. James, Duke of York, brother of Charles II, was then Lord High Admiral of England and he maintained his headquarters in Southwold's High Street.

In the Georgian era there was great unemployment in Suffolk. The textile industry had largely moved away and many Suffolk ports were too shallow to accommodate the newer, larger ships and thus lost trade. Gangs of armed and mounted smugglers dealt in alcohol and tea, terrorising law-abiding citizens. Nevertheless, some good Georgian architecture was built and a few towns like Bury St Edmunds and Bungay became spas.

From 1803 to 1812 coastal martello towers were built to deter a possible Napoleonic invasion. The idea came from Torre della Mortella, Corsica, where in 1794 a fortified tower defied two English warships. In Suffolk eighteen towers survive, typically 30 feet (9 metres) high and 40 feet (12 metres) in diameter. A small door high up in the tremendously thick walls led to the powder magazine and living quarters for thirty men with their howitzers and swivel guns. After the Napoleonic threat faded, the towers were used to subdue smugglers. Seven examples remain between Shingle Street and Felixstowe, but there is no public access.

Aldeburgh Martello Tower, Slaughden, Aldeburgh IP15 5NA (OS 156: TM 464549). Landmark Trust.
The property is readily accessible to the public though there is no internal access. Owners are the Landmark Trust, Shottesbrooke, Maidenhead, Berkshire SL6 3SW.

This large martello tower of stone-dressed yellow brickwork on a quatrefoil plan was completed in 1810 to house four heavy guns, with a battery of five twenty-five pounders which was swallowed by the sea in 1897, though part of the encircling wall remains, The sea wall was constructed after the 1953 floods, when the tower was in use as a house. It retains an impressive vaulted basement and stairs rising in the thickness of the external walls. The tower is rented out for self-catering holidays.

Bungay Castle, Bungay (OS 156: TM 332898). Telephone: 01986 893148.
Open daily.
Overlooking the river Waveney in the town

The massive twin towers of the gatehouse of Bungay Castle.

The impressive abbey ruins at Bury St Edmunds.

centre is the ruinous 70 feet (21 metres) square stone keep built by Roger Bigod in 1160, its walls reputedly amongst the thickest in England. The castle surrendered to the king in 1174, from which time the siege tunnel remains. The Bigods kept their ruin, paid a fine and in due course rebuilt it. Following a licence to crenellate, the upper walls were taken down in 1294 and the stone was used to build an encircling curtain wall with massive twin-towered gatehouse and swivelling drawbridge. Yet the castle was ruinous by 1382 and not much repaired until 1965.

Bury St Edmunds Abbey, Bury St Edmunds (OS 155: TL 859642). Telephone: 01284 764667.
Open daily.

The abbey church of St Edmundsbury grew from a small monastery founded around AD 633. Made significant by St Edmund's martyrdom, it grew into one of the most powerful and wealthy Benedictine monasteries in England. King Canute's twenty monks, installed in 1020, were increased by William the Conqueror to eighty in 1081 and there was a library of two thousand volumes. Then the church was rebuilt with a nave 50 feet (15 metres) longer than Norwich Cathedral and a west front wider than any English medieval church.

The abbey's precinct was enormous, including a palace yard, song school, cloisters, refectory, charnel house, dovecote, great court and chapter-house. The richly carved Norman gate, built in the 1130s, is now the bell-tower for the Cathedral Church of St James.

The abbey was burnt during riots in 1327, after which the Great Gate was erected; it now stands strong, battlemented and beautifully decorated on Angel Hill. It was a temporary reprieve, for at the Dissolution the abbey was sold for £412 and its stone quarried for new buildings; dwellings appeared even in the flint core walls of the west front beside Samson's Tower (page 102). The precinct now encompasses fine public gardens, amongst which lie massive flinty ruins and the site of the high altar, where the barons met in 1214 to plan Magna Carta.

Butley Priory Gatehouse, Butley, Woodbridge (OS 169: TM 377494). 6¹/₄ miles (10 km) east of Woodbridge.
No public access.

Butley Priory was founded in 1171 for the Austin canons by the founder of Leiston Abbey, Ranulph de Glanville. By 1200 there were thirty-six canons. Only a fragment survives of Butley Priory's fine church, but its flamboyant gatehouse of 1325 is complete, showing spectacular early flushwork decoration visible from the road. After the Dissolution it was bought by a Hadleigh clothier, later to become a hunting lodge.

Clare Castle, Clare, Sudbury (OS 155: Tl 768454). Telephone (warden): 01787 277491.
Open daily.

First mentioned in 1090, this stronghold commanded the Icknield Way, growing slowly into a keep on top of a 100 feet (30 metre) motte now ascended by a spiral path. The incentive to climb is the view over Clare, not the ruin, which has been quarried. Little remains of any buildings and the inner of the two baileys was from 1863 to 1967 astonishingly occupied by Clare railway station.

Clare Priory, Clare, Sudbury (OS 154: TL 768454).
Open daily.

Within the outer bailey of Clare Castle stand the remains of the first Augustinian house in England, founded in 1248. Nearby are the ruinous church, consecrated in 1338, the great cloister and the beautiful prior's house, rebuilt from the fourteenth century to the eighteenth. The present church, restored to the Augustinians in 1954, was originally two-storeyed, maybe a dormitory; it has a fine medieval roof.

Dunwich Greyfriars, Dunwich, Saxmundham (OS 156: TM 477701).
Open daily.

These are the clifftop remains of a Franciscan friary founded before 1277 but moved inland around 1290 after a storm. There was a refectory, cloister, nave, chancel and chapter-house, but demolition was so thorough after the Dissolution that only one building remains. It is now the centrepiece of a huge walled enclosure which is punctuated by two gateways, for the friary and for worshipping townspeople.

Eye Castle, Eye (OS 144: TM 147737).
Open Easter to September, daily.

Eye Castle, on its Norman motte, was probably strongest when rebuilt in 1182 after repulsing an attack by Hugh Bigod. After falling in 1265 it rapidly deteriorated and a post mill was built there in 1560. That was replaced in 1844 by a folly with cruciform openings, concealing a house for the batman of the owner, Sir Edward Kerrison, who had

Butley Priory Gatehouse was used as a hunting lodge.

Framlingham Castle was rebuilt in 1199 to the latest ideas in military fortifications.

saved his life at Waterloo. Damaged by a storm in the 1960s, the ruins provide a viewpoint over Eye.

Framlingham Castle, Framlingham IP13 3BP (OS 156: TM 285636). Telephone: 01728 723330. English Heritage.
Open throughout the year, but closed on Mondays from December to April.

The castle includes the Lanman Museum in the poor-house (page 105). A previous Framlingham Castle, built by Hugh Bigod, was dismantled by Henry II, but the resourceful Bigods redeemed it from the impoverished Richard the Lionheart, rebuilding it in Caen stone brought up the river Alde, which was dammed to create a defensive marsh.

The new castle was complete in 1199, when King John was crowned. As a result of intelligence from the Crusaders, it demonstrated the most advanced military thinking of the day: instead of a keep, thirteen projecting towers and a gatehouse were distributed around a tall fortified curtain wall.

Framlingham sheltered ambitious dukes and earls, attracting wealth, rebellion, siege and destruction. Royalty hunted in the deer park and Mary Tudor's supporters rallied here on her coronation in 1553. The Tudor brick chimneys, incongruous amongst the battlements, date from those hunting-lodge days, along with remains of a bridge which carried horses straight out into the surrounding park. Later, unco-operative priests were imprisoned here.

In 1635 Sir Robert Hitcham bought the castle, leaving it to Pembroke College, Cambridge, requiring all except the stone buildings to be pulled down and a workhouse, almshouse and school to be erected in the town. Visitors can walk along the battlemented curtain walls, below which the largest remaining building is the 1729 poor-house.

Landguard Fort, Felixstowe IP11 8TW (OS 169: TM 284319). 1¹/₄ miles (2 km) south of Felixstowe. English Heritage.

Reopening 1997, after renovation work.

The first Landguard Fort was completed in 1628, rebuffing a Dutch invasion in 1667. Continuing modification throughout the eighteenth century produced the pentagonal layout of battered brick walls and deep ditches visible today. In 1870 the old bastioned fort was transformed into a monumental casemated battery using granite slabs and wrought-iron shields. Yet warship ordnance progressed so quickly that it was soon out of date. Further batteries were added and by 1945 the original fort was almost surrounded by later accretions. In 1957 the army abandoned this massive enterprise, with its subterranean corridors, embrasures for tallow candles, elevating tackle for muzzle-loaders and gaunt concrete shapes.

Leiston Abbey, Leiston (OS 156: TM 444642). Telephone: 01728 830764. 1¼ miles (2 km) north of Leiston, off B1122. English Heritage.
Open daily.

This abbey was founded for Premonstratensian canons, who sought simplicity in secluded spots. They found one at Minsmere in 1182, rebuilding further from the sea on the present site in 1363 and again after a fire in 1382. Following the dissolution the abbey became a farm. Domestic accommodation was later constructed amongst extensive remains such as the cloister, presbytery and transepts of the abbey church. The adjacent great barn and Guesten Hall (which served the lay brothers) were restored in 1988 as a concert hall for the Pro Corda Trust.

Lindsey St James's Chapel, Lindsey, Ipswich (OS 155: TL 980444). 1¾ miles (3 km) east of Kersey. English Heritage.
Open daily.

This is a tiny Early English thatched chapel with lancet windows and some Tudor brickwork. Perhaps it was the chapel of the nearby motte and bailey castle, whose earthworks remain on private land.

Mettingham Castle, Mettingham, Bungay (OS 156: TM 359887). 1¼ miles (2 km) east of Bungay.

Not open to the public; view from roadside only.

In 1342 John de Norwich, one of Edward III's captains, castellated his residence and added a massive gateway and portcullis. It was converted to a well-endowed college in 1394, but only the fine flint gatehouse survives.

Orford Castle, Orford, Woodbridge IP12 2ND (OS 169: TM 419499). Telephone. 01394 450472. English Heritage.
Open daily.

Orford Castle was built in 1165-73 by Henry II to discourage coastal raiders and rebels. Under its shelter, the town's port was to be developed and surrounding marshes drained. Most of the original earthwork defences and curtain walls are long gone, but the surviving polygonal keep is a powerfully impressive structure offering a spectacular

The Tudor gatehouse visible through an archway at Leiston Abbey.

The keep of Orford Castle overlooks the town.

panorama from its 90 feet (27 metres) high rooftop. Inside the walls (which are thick enough to conceal passages) there are two great halls, a chapel and a great wheel stair winding down to the basement.

A medieval chronicler recorded that a merman, caught in fishermen's nets off Orford, was once detained here, naked, wild and hairy. Though he would eat raw fish, he refused to speak and eventually escaped back to the sea. Some say he later returned voluntarily to his captors.

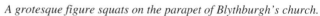

A grotesque figure squats on the parapet of Blythburgh's church.

6
Churches

Suffolk has a great density of churches, especially of those dating from medieval times. Dramatic flint towers, clerestories and timber roofs recall medieval power and wealth founded on cloth, fishing and trade.

Some forty round church towers of flint recall early watch-towers or strongpoints against coastal raiders, especially in the northeast, or armouries or treasuries. The tallest and thinnest is at Blundeston, the stumpiest at Wortham.

Most Suffolk churches date from the Perpendicular period (roughly 1330-1500) and are finished in flushwork – contrasting stone and patterned flint ornament. Such ambitious projects were funded by trade and fishing (for example, Covehithe, Southwold, Walberswick, Blythburgh), by profits from the cloth industry (Lavenham, Kersey, Long Melford), or by men enriched in war as military adventurers, plunderers and career soldiers (from the Hundred Years War and the Wars of the Roses). Churches were embellished as individual acts of piety to assure salvation and remembrance; legacies raised towers, clerestories and chapels. Imposing porches were built for penance, baptism and marriage. Existing churches were enlarged, often radically, giving magnificent opportunities for roofs of local oak decorated with wooden angels, fine furnishings and brasses. Fonts, covered to safeguard hallowed water from witches, were beautifully carved with scenes from scripture and daily life, as were pews when they were installed from the fifteenth century to assist preaching.

Wall-paintings illustrated religious themes and the 'cult of the rood' raised brightly coloured screens as objects of veneration, inviting yet more imposing naves. Then in the 1530s came Henry VIII's ban on 'superstitious practices', ultimately removing roodscreens (depicting Christ on the Cross) so that hardly a single one survived. Wall-paintings, especially those of the Virgin Mary, were obscured and other works of art lost, to reappear in the twentieth century. The most famous of these is the Thornham Parva Retable, painted around 1300.

There was a temporary reversal under Catholic Queen Mary I, but Elizabeth I's succession in 1558 firmly established the Protestant Church of England; recusants who refused to conform were fined or, after 1580, locked up in the keep of Framlingham Castle. Rood lofts were turned into beds or weavers' looms or burnt to melt lead for the church roof. Some destruction was averted, as when carved font panels were merely plastered over, or rood-loft stairs only blocked up. Some stained glass, as at Long Melford, was quietly taken down and stored, giving authority the impression of compliance. St Mary, Mendlesham, safeguards another relic from this era: the village armour, provided for the Armada emergency of 1588.

In the seventeenth century the despoiled churches began to revive: there was a flowering of beautiful pulpits. Then came the 1640 Long Parliament and Cromwellian puritanism. Many angel roofs, previously unscathed, bear scars from this period. A Parliamentary edict of 1641 encouraged William Dowsing, a 'Parliamentary Visitor', to sweep through 150 Suffolk churches in less than fifty days in 1643. At Clare a thousand sacred images were destroyed, at Bramford 841, at Covehithe two hundred, at Hadleigh seventy; these included fonts, carvings, paintings, ornaments, altars and pulpits.

After William and Mary acceded to the throne in 1688 nonconformity was established in the 1689 Act of Toleration and chapels were built all over Suffolk, recalling the Lollards from Beccles and Bungay who had sought reform in the fifteenth century.

The Victorian period brought many modifications, peaking around 1860 when 'restoration' changed the character of many more active churches. Old timber fittings were replaced in new pine; thatch gave way to slate; organs were added; galleries and box pews were removed. Some changes were inspired by dogma: for example, the Tractarians or 'Oxford Movement' sought greater ritual, so steps were installed and chancel floors raised and surfaced with Minton tiles. Vigorous new churches emulated medieval carpentry or used new materials like encaustic tiles and contemporary stained glass.

Barsham with Shipmeadow: Holy Trinity. (On B1062, 1³/₄ miles, 3 km, west of Beccles.)

The church has a Saxon flint round tower and a new thatched nave roof, rebuilt after a fire in 1979. Most dramatic is the diagonal stone patterning of the east gable. The pulpit and roodscreen are partly Jacobean, the painted canopy early twentieth-century, when the chancel roof was decorated. There are poppyhead bench ends with beasts and birds, a square Purbeck marble font and memorials to the Suckling family.

Blythburgh: Holy Trinity. (Off A12, 3 miles, 5 km, west of Southwold.)

This is a splendid church, dominant over deserted marshes, floodlit at night. The long, clerestoried nave with excellent flushwork was added around 1475 to a 1330 tower, which had a spire until its collapse in the sixteenth century. During the Civil War horses were stabled in the spacious light interior and now an annual animal service is held there. The celebrated angel roof includes coloured patterns of stencilled flowers and monograms. Bench-end figures include Sloth in bed, Drunkenness in the stocks, Avarice sitting on a money chest, and harvesting and pig killing. Also note the 1682 clock jack and the priest's room over the south porch.

Boxford: St Mary. (Off A1071 between Sudbury and Hadleigh.)

St Mary has a good carved tower and unusual timbered north porch from the early fourteenth century. The south porch is late Perpendicular. Wall-paintings include a Doom and a Richard II mural. There is a curious hinged font cover and a tablet to a woman, four times widowed, who died aged 113 in 1738. The east window was inserted in 1972.

Braiseworth: St Mary. (East of A140, 1¹/₄ miles, 2 km, south-west of Eye.)

This Norman church was rebuilt in 1857 by E. B. Lamb, who incorporated the old south door into his neo-Norman west elevation. Small groups of windows, mannered, chamfered and unusually decorated, culminate in strange dormers and a crowning bellcote. The twelfth-century chancel from the old church is a churchyard mortuary chapel.

Bramfield: St Andrew. (On A144, 1³/₄ miles, 3 km, south of Halesworth.)

St Andrew is notable for its freestanding flint round tower near the colourwashed, thatched nave. Internally, the fine timber screen from around 1500 retains traces of red, green, blue and gold decoration. Alabaster sculpture by Nicholas Stone shows Dame Elizabeth Coke lying on her pillow with babe in arms and husband kneeling. Rabbit heads are carved in the memorials of the Rabett family. Opposite the church is a good crinkle-crankle wall.

Bury St Edmunds: St Edmundsbury Cathedral. Telephone: 01284 754933.

The mother church of Suffolk was mostly built in 1503-39, partly by the architect of King's College, Cambridge. It became a cathedral in 1914. There are fine stained glass windows below a brightly decorated nave roof of hammerbeams and angels, reconstructed in 1862 by Sir George Gilbert Scott. Beyond the crossing are the Lady Chapel, St Edmund's Chapel and a beautifully roofed quire, built in 1964-70 to designs by Stephen Dykes-Bower. The refectory, song school and treasury were added in the 1990s.

Bury St Edmunds: St Mary, Honey Hill.

This was part of the huge abbey complex on the site of the Saxon minster. The fine porch features a flat panelled stone ceiling showing angels attending God. The magnificent nave roof includes wallposts and cornices carved with unicorns, dragons, fishes and angels. At one end, the John Baret

The magnificent church roof at Needham Market.

Chantry has a dramatic gilded and mirrored 'Canopy of Honour' roof dating from 1467.

Bury St Edmunds: Unitarian Meeting House, Churchgate Street.

This exuberant composition was built in 1711 in the style of Sir Christopher Wren in red brick with rubbed brick trimmings. Inside are a three-decker pulpit and box pews.

Covehithe: St Andrew (redundant). (East of A12, 3³/₄ miles, 6 km, north of Southwold.)

Built in the early fifteenth century, this church became too big to maintain, so in 1672 it was dismantled by parishioners, except for the tower. That remained as a seamark, together with some of the buttressed nave walls. Proceeds from the sale of the materials paid for the present small thatched church within part of the original nave arcade, giving a splendid if poignant composition. (Compare with Walberswick.)

Dennington: St Mary the Virgin. (On A1120, 1³/₄ miles, 3 km, north of Framlingham.)

The fascinating interior includes carved benches from 1525 which illustrate such curiosities as Skiapodes (a creature sheltering under its huge feet). Later and plainer Georgian box pews date from 1765. There is a Stuart reading desk and three-decker pulpit, a font with a painted pyramidal cover and beautiful coloured tracery screens to the chantry chapels. Lord Bardolph of Agincourt, a colleague of Henry V, founded the colourful St Margaret's Chapel in 1437, shortly before he died; note his alabaster tomb.

Denston: St Nicholas. (East of A143, north-east of Haverhill.)

St Nicholas is a fine small church largely unchanged since its reconstruction as a collegiate chapel *c.*1475. The arcaded lofty interior is notable for carvings on cornices and nave benches of hares, hounds, lions, harts and crocodiles. Also note a Seven Sacraments font, box pews, medieval glazed tiles and medieval glass in the east window depicting a strutting bird.

Ellough: All Saints (redundant). (Off A145, south-east of Beccles.)

This simple church stands alone on a bleak site with a large churchyard, its imposing tower dating from about 1300. In the 1880s the floor was tiled, pine benches installed and an organ chamber added during a restoration, possibly by William Butterfield, which ranged from the 1602 porch to the handsome cambered tiebeam roof of about 1450 which was reinforced with wallposts on head corbels.

The ruins of Covehithe's huge church, in which its tiny successor stands.

Elveden: St Andrew and St Patrick. (On A11, south-west of Thetford.)

This illustrates six hundred years of church architecture around a Norman nave. The west tower was added in the 1420s, to be remodelled in 1869 by Maharajah Duleep Singh. Then in 1904-22 Lord Iveagh engaged W. D. Caroe to add another nave containing an elaborate pulpit and organ case, a new chancel with alabaster reredos and, in 1922, a second, highly decorated tower connected to the existing church by an equally decorated arcade. All the latter work is Art Nouveau Gothic in style, with stained glass by Kempe and Brangwyn.

Euston: St Genevieve. (Off A1088, southeast of Thetford, and within Euston Park.)

This classical church was largely rebuilt on medieval foundations by the Earl of Arlington in 1676, becoming 'one of the prettiest country churches in England' (John Evelyn). It compares well with Wren's contemporary City churches; note the vaulted nave with ornamental plasterwork, wainscoting, carving and box pews below circular clerestory windows.

Eye: St Peter and St Paul. (East of A140, south-east of Diss.)

The dramatic west tower, built in 1460-84, is 101 feet (31 metres) high, panelled top to bottom in flushwork. The ground floor is fanvaulted. Above it a gallery opens to the nave. The two-stage south porch includes a stone shelf for charity loaves. Inside, the carved and gilded screen from the 1470s was restored in 1929 by Sir Ninian Comper.

Felixstowe: St Andrew, St Andrew's Road.

This elegantly detailed 1930s modern church was designed by Hilda Mason and Raymond Erith but built without its tower. The spacious porch leads to an interior where silvery grey concrete columns and open spandrels evoke the sensibility of old oak. There are tall leaded windows of obscured glass and a parquet floor.

Framlingham: St Michael the Archangel.

This church has a powerful tower patterned in flushwork stars and wheels below lion battlements. Under the splendid hammerbeam roof, choir stalls show traceried bench ends which were once cut in half and used as floor joists; frames of old box pews line the aisle walls. About 1554 the chancel was lengthened and vast side chapels were added to house magnificent tombs of the Catholic Howard family, Dukes of Norfolk. The south chancel aisle contains the altar tomb of Sir Robert Hitcham, great benefactor of Framlingham, and the fine reredos displays a 'Glory' centrepiece. The decorated pipes of the galleried 1674 baroque organ produce a wonderful 'Great Chorus'.

Fressingfield. St Peter and St Paul. (On B1116, south of Harleston.)

Fressingfield church is entered by a lovely flushwork south porch, battlemented, with a first-floor chamber. Lofty tower arches allow the west window to flood daylight into the nave below a low-pitched single hammerbeam oak roof. Magnificent benches with traceried ends and buttressed arm rests show emblems of Christ's passion and the initials of Alice de la Pole, Chaucer's granddaughter, who married a Duke of Suffolk. There is fine 1890s stained glass by Henry Holiday. Bordering the churchyard is the Fox and Goose inn, originally the guildhall.

Gipping: St Nicholas. (East of B1113, 3 miles, 5 km, north of Stowmarket.)

This church was built in 1483 by Sir James Tyrell as a private chapel beside a mansion, which is now demolished. The buttressed walls of chequered flint and stone, with flushwork decoration of monograms and heraldic devices including the Tyrell knot, are dominated by beautiful windows which flood the interior with light. Fragments of original glass remain in the east window: note the peacock's tail in a boar's mouth. The rendered tower is Victorian.

Great Finborough: St Andrew. (On B1115, 1¾ miles, 3 km, west of Stowmarket.)

Between 1874 and 1877 no expense was spared on this design by R. M. Phipson. A tall west tower supports an upper octagonal stage leading to a slender spire, with the

Above: *One of the angels in the hammerbeam roof at St Mary's church, Huntingfield.*

Left: *A roof panel in St Margaret's, Ipswich, celebrating the accession of William and Mary.*

Below: *The alabaster tomb of Lord and Lady Bardolph in Dennington church.*

Wenhaston church's Doom painting.

Above left: *Flint and stone walls are pierced by fine windows at St Nicholas's church, Gipping.*

Above right: *A detail of the stained glass in the east window of St Margaret's, Herringfleet.*

octagonal belfry on flying buttresses. There is abundant sculpture with grotesque masks amidst the flushwork. Phipson also designed the conspicuous spire of nearby St Mary, Woolpit.

Herringfleet: St Margaret. (On B1074, 4¹/₄ miles, 7 km, north-west of Lowestoft.)

This is a small thatched church with a flint round tower and Norman entrance. Wonderful kaleidoscopic stained glass windows show a collage of heraldic arms, biblical scenes and geometric patterns spanning four centuries. These were inserted in the 1820s, brought from several buildings in Cologne by Henry Leathes, who went there after fighting at Waterloo. Also note the inscriptions on the porch benches.

Hessett: St Ethelbert. (South of A14, east of Bury St Edmunds.)

An inscription states that John Hoo (died 1492) built the north aisle, raised the vestry and made battlements with openwork carv-ings. Inside, faded wall-paintings show the Seven Deadly Sins and Christ of the Trades with medieval tools. Stained glass depicts medieval scenes. Two of the church's great treasures, the fifteenth-century pyx cloth and corporas case, both of linen lace, are now in the British Museum.

Huntingfield: St Mary. (Off B1117, 3 miles, 5 km, south-west of Halesworth.)

The most remarkable feature of this church is the medieval hammerbeam angel roof which was splendidly repainted in vibrant colours *c*.1860 by Mildred Keyworth Holland, the rector's wife, including large carvings of saints and ornamental decoration. There is also an interesting memorial to John Paston, who died in 1575, and a chapel for the Vanneck family which is now an organ chamber.

Icklingham: All Saints. (On A1101, 3³/₄ miles, 6 km, east of Mildenhall.)

On an ancient religious site, this now redundant church was modified in the fifteenth century but abandoned when the village moved away. The nave is Norman (later extended), with a reed-thatched roof visible inside and a tall square chalky flint tower. The fine lofty clear interior contains a medieval tiled floor, stained glass, backless pews and good stone carving.

Ipswich: St Margaret, St Margaret's Green.

St Margaret presides over Christchurch Park and St Margaret's Plain. Inside, the excellent late fifteenth-century double hammerbeam roof was decorated in 1695 with painted panels celebrating peace after the Glorious Revolution of 1688 (the iron ties were inserted in 1800). Angels hacked off the hammerbeams were replaced in 1700 with the emblems of Ipswich families.

Ipswich: Unitarian Meeting House, Friars Street.

This early nonconformist chapel was built by the carpenter Joseph Clarke only a decade after the 1689 Toleration Act, so a surviving spyhole in the east door is no surprise. A dignified plaster front with an oval window leads into a timbered interior where giant Tuscan columns support the roof. The carved pulpit is a focus to the box pews and large gallery and the whole composition recalls the New England churches set up by emigrating East Anglians of the 1630s.

Kedington: St Peter and St Paul. (Off B1061, 1¾ miles, 3 km, north-east of Haverhill.)

Known as the 'Westminster Abbey of Suffolk', this church contains the monuments from 1503 to 1724 of the Barnardiston family, who were puritan leaders in the 1660s. The three-decker Jacobean pulpit with tester has an hourglass stand and wig-pole for the parson. The wood carvings are superb and the nave piers are painted to appear fluted. Medieval graffiti depict a ship and sword.

Lakenheath: St Mary. (On B1112, north of Mildenhall.)

St Mary comprises a Norman chancel with lancet window and a tower built of limestone chalk, ironstone, Tudor red brick and flint. Inside, the dark wood hammerbeam roof carries large angels, wings outspread, which were restored in the early twentieth century. There are wall-paintings of St Edmund and the Life of Christ and an early font with a good modern cover. Bench ends from the 1480s include a unicorn, an elephant and a harvester.

Lavenham: St Peter and St Paul. (On A1141, south-east of Bury St Edmunds.)

Completed in 1525, this is an outstanding late Perpendicular church which was funded by the Earl of Oxford and the Springs, a

The Unitarian Meeting House in Ipswich was built in 1699.

Fishing boats on the beach at Aldeburgh.

Bawdsey beach.

Sunset over the river Alde.

Holy Trinity, Long Melford, is one of the finest of all Perpendicular churches.

family of local clothiers who intermarried with the Earl's family. Ironically, Lavenham's prosperity ended shortly after the church was finished. The tower is 141 feet (43 metres) high, of knapped flint decorated with stars, shields, the keys of St Peter and the swords of St Paul; at its base the walls are 7 feet (2.1 metres) thick. The stone-faced nave has twelve clerestory windows and a spectacular fan-vaulted porch and there are beautiful screens to the Spring Chantry and Oxford Chantry. The carved misericords include a pelican and a jester.

Leiston: St Mary of Antioch.

The simple Perpendicular tower was the only element kept in E. B. Lamb's 1853 rebuilding: the church was too small for the flourishing industrial town. Flint walls are dressed with bands of Kentish ragstone and Caen stone; they are low, throwing across the nave a soaring roof rising at the crossing into a dramatic Gothic Revival composition.

Long Melford: Holy Trinity. (West of A134, north of Sudbury.)

This is a fine Perpendicular church in flushwork on a stone plinth, mainly funded by the Clopton family (who were given Kentwell Hall after the dissolution of Bury Abbey and who are illustrated in a north aisle window). Eighteen clerestory windows show the names of their donors; one window depicts three rabbits sharing three ears, symbolising the Trinity. Another window shows the Duchess of Norfolk who became Tenniel's model for the Duchess in *Alice in Wonderland*. The original tower was struck by lightning in 1709 and its brick replacement encased in flint and stone about 1900. The beautifully carved Clopton Chantry, a small chapel cloistered on four sides with a central tomb, was built about 1500, but Clopton abandoned it for the Lady Chapel because his wife died before it was consecrated.

Lound: St John. (West of A12, 4¼ miles, 7 km, north-west of Lowestoft.)

Sir Ninian Comper boldly revitalised a number of church interiors, such as this 'golden church', refitted in 1912-15 with an exquisite roodscreen, high altar and font cover. In his wall-painting of St Christopher, Comper apparently depicted himself driving a Rolls-Royce; a restoration of 1964 added an aeroplane!

Mildenhall: St Mary.

An ambitious church 168 feet (51 metres) long, St Mary has a tower 120 feet (37 metres) high. The chancel and north chapel date from 1240, the remarkable seven-light east window from 1300. Above the nave are a host of carved angels, some damaged by black shot, iconoclasts' arrows and an axe. The north aisle roof shows St George, the dragon and imps playing an organ. In the tower a choir gallery opens on to the nave, and on the south wall is a huge set of George II arms dated 1758.

Needham Market: St John the Baptist. (On B1113, south east of Stowmarket.)

Rebuilt in flint around 1490, this has been a parish church only since 1907. It rises from the street without a churchyard; for centuries the dead were carried along the Causeway for burial in Barking. The exterior, with a slated spirelet and curious rooftop extension, little prepares one for the magnificent interior with its outstanding hammerbeam roof, built around 1475 and subsequently restored. Spanning 30 feet (9 metres) and bedecked with flying angels, it appears to float above the nave.

Newmarket: St Agnes, Bury Road.

St Agnes was designed by R. H. Carpenter in 1886 for the Duchess of Montrose in memory of her husband. The simple brick exterior belies a sumptuous interior with barely a hundred seats. Majolica, mosaic and lavish ceramic decoration provide some of the richest High Victorian church decoration in Suffolk. The stained glass is by Clayton & Bell; the marble reredos showing the Assumption is by Boehm; the organ was designed by Sir Arthur Sullivan.

Orford: St Bartholomew. (On B1084, east of Woodbridge.)

Two bold arcades and part of the crossing remain from the fine Norman chancel begun in 1166. The rest of the church is fourteenth-century with a high broad nave and a tower which partly collapsed in 1830, to be restored in 1972. The font is carved with lions and wild men. The first performances of Britten's *Noye's Fludde* (1958) and *Curlew River* (1964) took place in this church.

Rushbrooke: St Nicholas. (East of A134, 2½ miles, 4 km, south east of Bury St Edmunds.)

St Nicholas is a rendered brick church with crow-stepped gables. The curious interior was rearranged by Robert Rushbrooke (1779-1845), an 'amateur Victorian craftsman' who stripped panelling, maybe from Rushbrooke Hall, reassembling it in the church together with a painted organ and a possibly unique set of royal arms of Henry VIII. There are monuments to the Jermyn family, a fine roof and interesting stained glass.

A detail of the gilded canopy by Sir Ninian Comper in Lound church.

Left: *Leman House in Ballygate, Beccles, is occupied by the town's museum.*

Below: *Heveningham Hall has the finest frontage in the county.*

Kentwell Hall.

Ickworth House.

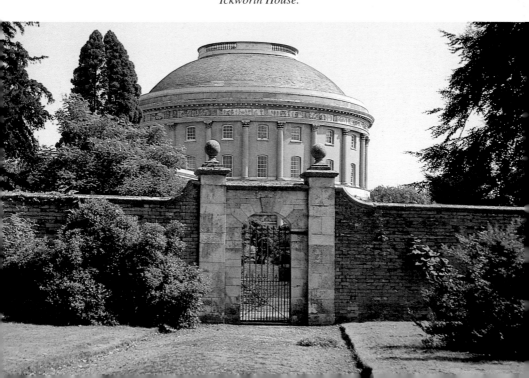

Southwold: St Edmund.

A large church with excellent flushwork, St Edmund was rebuilt around 1450 after a fire, with a hammerbeam angel roof and a colourful chancel. Painted screens separate traceried stalls from the chapels of Our Lady and Holy Trinity. Southwold Jack is a fifteenth-century wooden clock-striker in Yorkist uniform.

Stowlangtoft: St George. (East of A1088, north-east of Bury St Edmunds.)

This small Perpendicular church was built around 1400 by Robert Davey de Ashfield, 'a servant to the Black Prince', with chequered flushwork, spirited gargoyles and tall windows, but no finials or battlements. In-

A squirrel sits on a pew end at St George's church, Stowlangtoft.

side, the wall-painting of St Christopher with lobster, otter and fishing hermit is no longer decipherable, but magnificent wood carvings remain: sixty traceried bench ends include many animals and there are excellent misericords and a Flemish carved oak reredos depicting Christ's Passion. The iron strapwork door to the tower is notable, as are the brightly painted organ pipes from the 1851 Great Exhibition.

Sudbury: St Gregory on the Croft.

This is an imposing collegiate church much rebuilt in 1370 under the direction of Simon Teobald (1317-81), or Simon of Sudbury, who became Archbishop of Canterbury in 1375, crowning Richard II. As Chancellor of England in 1380 he introduced the poll tax to finance war with France. That, together with the arrival of the Black Death, sparked Wat Tyler's Peasants' Revolt of 1381. Teobald was killed by a mob on Tower Hill, London, and his pickled head can be viewed in this church; his body is buried at Canterbury. Note the lovely font cover and, in several locations, the heraldic talbot badge of Simon. He and his brother founded a college of canons, of which only the gateway remains, to the west of the church.

Walberswick: St Andrew. (On B1387, south of Southwold.)

A fine tower was added to the existing building in 1426, with further extensions until 1507, giving a stately, clerestoried church. Then came a downturn in fishing and shipbuilding, the loss of quay duties and various fires. In 1695 the townspeople capitulated and part demolished the nave, chancel and north aisle, selling off the lead and beams to raise £293 to rebuild the south aisle. Now there is a plain light interior and flagged aisle – no brasses remain – with medieval pulpit and defaced font.

Wenhaston: St Peter. (South of B1123, 2½ miles, 4 km, south-east of Halesworth.)

Wenhaston's Doom, on a wooden panel 17 feet (5.2 metres) wide by 8 feet 6 inches (2.6 metres) high, may have been painted by a monk from Blythburgh Priory c.1480. It

The round tower at Wortham is the largest in England.

was whitewashed over by 1545 and left, eventually to be put out in the churchyard in 1892. Rain revealed a dramatic scene of the Day of Judgement, which was restored in 1970.

Wingfield: St Andrew. (North of B1118, south-east of Diss.)

St Andrew is a collegiate church founded by Sir John Wingfield in 1361 and extended by Michael de la Pole (died 1415). Window tracery from 1362 includes the carved heads of John and Eleanor Wingfield each side of the south doorway. Inside, a canopied altar tomb shelters alabaster effigies of John de la Pole, Duke of Suffolk and Knight of the Garter, and his wife, Elizabeth Plantagenct.

Woodbridge: St Mary.

The church is well placed at the top of Church Street, with an alternative access from Market Hill. Its lavish tower and porch, built in the early fifteenth century, are covered in excellent flushwork with dense black flints. There was a priory on the site in the twelfth century. The original roodscreen, given in 1444 by the weaver John Albrede, must have been spectacular with over thirty painted panels; some remain on display in an aisle chapel (the present screen is Victorian). R. M. Phipson remodelled the interior in the 1870s, removing galleries and box pews and relocating the 1587 tomb of Thomas Seckford (see page 53) from his own chapel. Note the 1627 monument to the local tanner and haberdasher Geoffrey Pitman.

Wortham: St Mary. (North of A143, south-west of Diss.)

This has been called 'the most gaunt and uncouth church in Suffolk'. Its Norman round tower, 29 feet (8.8 metres) in diameter, is the largest in England and open to the sky since the top of the tower fell in 1780; there is a small timbered bell turret. The splendid pew ends, carved in the 1890s by a local man, Albert Bartrum, were inspired by Psalm 104. One rector became a highwayman; another, Richard Cobbold, wrote in 1845 the story of Margaret Catchpole.

Basketmaking at West Stow Anglo-Saxon Village. (Courtesy of St Edmundsbury Borough Council/West Stow Anglo-Saxon Village Trust.)

7
Historic buildings and gardens

Akenfield, 1 Park Lane, Charsfield, Woodbridge IP13 7PT. Telephone: 01473 37402.
Open April to October, daily.
Akenfield is a half-acre (0.2 hectare) council-house garden well stocked with flowers and vegetables.

Blakenham Woodland Garden, Little Blakenham, Ipswich. Telephone: 01473 830344. 3 1/4 miles (6 km) north-west of Ipswich.
Open March to June, daily except Saturdays.
This 5 acre (2 hectare) garden has many unusual trees and shrubs, including azaleas, camellias, rhododendrons and roses. The bluebell wood is spectacular in spring.

Bridge Cottage, Flatford, East Bergholt, Colchester CO7 6UL. Telephone: 01206 298260. 1 1/4 miles (2 km) south of East Bergholt. National Trust.
Open: April, May and October, Wednesdays to Sundays; June to September, daily.
Near Flatford Mill, this sixteenth-century thatched cottage, featured in several of John Constable's paintings, contains a display about the artist.

Bury St Edmunds Abbey Gardens, Bury St Edmunds.
Former botanic gardens, with elaborate floral displays, beside the river Lark, include the Appleby Rose Garden.

Euston Hall, Thetford IP24 2OW. Telephone: 01842 766366. 5 miles (8 km) north of Ixworth, off A1088.
Open June to September, Thursday afternoons and some Sundays.
Euston Hall occupies the site of a medieval manor house. The present building dates from around 1666, when the estate was purchased by the Earl of Arlington, Secretary of State to the newly restored King Charles II; his daughter married the first Duke of Grafton, whose descendants still live here. The house, then in French style, was modified around 1745 when Matthew Brettingham replaced the corner domes with pyramidal roofs. A fire in 1902 ultimately led to further modifications in the 1930s. The interiors include paintings and family portraits by Van Dyck, Stubbs and Lely. The landscaped park around the house was designed by John Evelyn and 'Capability' Brown and includes an octagonal temple by William Kent and a church (page 83).

Guildhall of Corpus Christi, Market Place, Lavenham. See page 106.

Hadleigh Guildhall, Hadleigh. Telephone: 01473 827752.
Open May to September, Thursday and Sunday afternoons. Groups are welcome at other times, by arrangement.
The fine colourwashed timber-framed building facing St Mary's church and known as the Guildhall was originally several separate buildings. In 1438 William de Clopton gave 'the market house, newly built long house, almshouses, shops and priest's chambers' to the town. The five Hadleigh guilds (Corpus Christi, Trinity, Our Lady, Jesus and St John's) used a hall a short distance away. Towards the end of the fifteenth century a first-floor hall with a fine crown-post roof was built over the guildroom, joining the buildings. Over the centuries the building has been much changed and put to many uses: it has served as a workhouse, school, assembly room and corset factory. Following a major refurbishment programme com-

pleted in 1994, it provides five halls which are used for public and private functions, dances, plays, meetings, exhibitions etc and also houses Hadleigh Town Council.

Haughley Park, Haughley, Stowmarket IP14 3JY. Telephone: 01359 240205. 3 miles (5 km) north-west of Stowmarket.
Open May to September, Tuesday afternoons.

Haughley Park was built around 1620 by the Sulyard family as a Jacobean 'E' plan manor house, which was given a new garden front *c*.1800. It was damaged by fire in 1961 and much of the interior dates from the subsequent restoration. It is set amongst gardens and woodland with a notable seventeenth-century barn sometimes used for lectures.

Helmingham Hall Gardens, Helmingham, Stowmarket IP14 6EF. Telephone: 01473 890363. 3³/₄ miles (6 km) south of Debenham.
Open late April to early September, Sunday afternoons.

Although the house is not open to the public, the gardens extend to the brink of its moat, from which the drawbridge is still regularly raised. From there a Tudor brick gateway leads on to the hall range. About 1750 the old timber-framed walls were faced with brick and fifty years later John Nash gothicised them, replacing windows, adding buttresses, finials and battlements. Finally in 1840 Anthony Salvin remodelled the west front in Revivalist Tudor style, copying many earlier features.

The extensive gardens of this family home include an ancient deer park, parkland with an obelisk, moated gardens, a walled garden, a knot garden and a notable rose garden. At the gates is an estate village of steep-gabled houses, each with a one acre (0.4 hectare) smallholding.

St Mary's church has a fine collection of memorials of the Tollemache family who own Helmingham Hall.

Hengrave Hall, Hengrave, Bury St Edmunds IP28 6LZ. Telephone: 01284 701561. 1³/₄ miles (3 km) north-west of Bury St Edmunds.
Open by prior appointment.

Now a conference and retreat centre, Hengrave Hall was built in brick and stone in 1525 for Thomas Kytson, a rich cloth merchant, who was knighted in 1533. The Renaissance carved south front, inner court and later Victorian banqueting hall are all noteworthy; the intricate, turreted entrance is magnificent. There were extensive alterations in the eighteenth century and much of the interior is Edwardian, but the oratory retains glass from the early sixteenth century depicting biblical scenes.

England's finest madrigal writer, John Wilbye (1574-1638), was resident musician here from 1592 to 1628.

Heveningham Hall, Heveningham. 3³/₄ miles (6 km) south-west of Halesworth, off B1117.
Not open to the public, but the mansion and its parkland, lake, icehouse and gate-lodges are all visible from the road and public footpath.

Set in a 'Capability' Brown landscape, this grandest of the county's country houses was designed around 1778 by Sir Robert Taylor for Sir Gerard Vanneck, but the glorious interior, finished in 1784, is James Wyatt's. In recent years the government has squandered an opportunity to buy this wonderful house for the nation and it is now privately owned. There are plans to reinstate the park to the original design.

Hintlesham Hall, Hintlesham, near Ipswich. Telephone: 01473 652334. 3³/₄ miles (6 km) west of Ipswich, off A1071.
Open as a hotel.

Begun in 1570 by the Timperley family, extensive areas of Elizabethan brickwork are still visible behind the dramatic new classical façade which was applied around 1725. This introduced coloured render, quoins, rustication and an entrance portico. Inside, there are lovely plaster ceilings and an oak staircase.

Ickworth House, Garden and Park, Horringer, Bury St Edmunds IP29 5QE. Telephone: 01284 735270. 2¹/₂ miles (4 km) south-west of Bury St Edmunds, off A143. National Trust.
Park and garden open daily. House open from late March to early November, daily except Mondays and Thursdays. Closed Good Friday.

This extraordinary oval house with curved

flanking wings was created by the Earl of Bristol (1764-1830), who was also appointed Bishop of Derry. The stuccoed brick frontage is some 700 feet (213 metres) long. It was first intended that the eccentric Earl would live in the domed rotunda and use the wings for art treasures which had been collected on the Grand Tour, but when Napoleon entered Italy the Earl's collection was confiscated and he died without seeing his building completed. Now it is well furnished and hung with paintings by Titian, Velasquez and Gainsborough, and there is Georgian silver.

The park, designed by 'Capability' Brown, extends over 1800 acres (728 hectares) and contains fine oak pollards from ancient woodland, a walled garden with a 1718 greenhouse and Victorian formal gardens including an Italian garden. The obelisk was erected in 1804; there are woodland walks, a deer enclosure and adventure playground. Leaflets are available in the car park describing a 7 mile (11 km) walk through the park.

Kentwell Hall, Long Melford, Sudbury CO10 9BA. Telephone: 01787 310207.
Open usually daily in the afternoon.

A great lime avenue planted in 1678 leads to the imposing house, which dates from the sixteenth century. The moats and main elevations are of a similar age but internally much has been altered, principally by Thomas Hopper in the 1820s, creating some fine rooms with magnificent use of plaster to simulate woodwork. Since 1971 the house has been enthusiastically restored and a farm has been built, resulting in regular 'historical recreations' of Tudor life. The many attractions extend outside to a rose garden, maze, woodland walks and in the walled garden a potager and extensive herb garden.

Little Hall, Market Place, Lavenham, Sudbury CO10 9QZ. Telephone: 01787 247179.
Open Easter to October, Wednesday to Sunday.

This lovely hall-house dates from the fourteenth century and retains its solar, diamond-mullioned windows and exposed timber frame. The later-inserted dormitory provides a good view of the fine crown-post roof, which still shows smoke blackening from an open-hearth fire. Many of the alterations to the house reflect Lavenham's history. In the 1920s the building appeared flush-fronted, rendered and of uncertain age, but a 1930s restoration revealed its glories. Since 1974 it has been the headquarters of the Suffolk Preservation Society and Suffolk Building Preservation Trust and contains the Gayer-Anderson collection of furniture, sculpture and ceramics. There is also a fine garden.

Melford Hall, Long Melford, Sudbury CO10 9AH. Telephone: 01787 371394. National Trust.
Open: April to October, weekends; also Wednesdays and Thursdays from May to September.

Screened from Long Melford's huge green

The fifteenth-century Otley Hall.

by a tall front wall with arched gateway, this pepperpot-turreted red-brick Tudor mansion was commenced in 1578 when Sir William Cordell entertained Queen Elizabeth I. Here are shades of Hampton Court, extended in Georgian times. Within, see the original panelled banqueting hall, Regency library and a good collection of Chinese porcelain from a Spanish galleon captured in 1762. There is also an exhibition celebrating Beatrix Potter's visits here. In the gardens note the octagonal gazebo.

Otley Hall, Otley, Ipswich IP6 9PA. Telephone: 01473 890264. 6 miles (9 km) northwest of Woodbridge.
Public open days advertised locally. Open to groups by appointment.
Otley Hall is a fine fifteenth-century moated house, still a family home, set in 10 acres (4 hectares) of gardens and grounds, with many features of architectural and historical interest, such as sixteenth-century frescoes, linenfold panelling, pargeting and herringbone brickwork.

The Priory, Water Street, Lavenham, Sudbury CO10 9RW. Telephone 01787 247003.
Open: Easter, May and Late Spring bank holiday weekends; late July to early September, daily.
This timber-framed building housed a Benedictine priory which by 1600 had been transformed into a clothier's hall-house. Pargeting and wall-paintings remain, as well as a Jacobean staircase and modern stained glass. The gardens include a pond, an orchard and a varied collection of herbs.

Pykenham's Gatehouse, Northgate Street, Ipswich IP1 3BU. Telephone contact: 01473 255591.
Open May to December, only on the first and third Saturday morning each month.
This is the restored gatehouse to the Archdeacon of Suffolk's residence in Ipswich. It was built in 1471 and is full of

The tower of the main garden front of Somerleyton Hall.

architectural interest.

Seckford Hall, Woodbridge. Half a mile (1 km) south of Woodbridge, off A12.
Open as a hotel.
The long red-brick Tudor frontage with gables, fine chimneys and brick mullioned windows dates from the late sixteenth century but was much restored and partially rebuilt in the 1940s and has later been extended. It was probably linked with the father of Thomas Seckford (page 53).

Somerleyton Hall, Somerleyton, Lowestoft NR32 5QQ. Telephone: 01502 730224. 3³/₄ miles (6 km) north-west of Lowestoft, off B1074.
Open Easter to end of September, Sundays, Thursdays and bank holidays; also Tuesdays and Wednesdays in July and August.
This Elizabethan hall was bought in 1844 and magnificently transformed in seven years by Sir Samuel Morton Peto, the Victorian tycoon who was a railway contractor in Buenos Aires, Algiers and East Suffolk and MP for Norwich. Somerleyton has been described as 'pandemonium in red brick', though there is abundant masonry in stone from Caen and Aubigny, carved with strapwork patterns. The eclectic style incorporates Palladian, Jacobean

The eighteenth-century façade of Wingfield Old College.

and Italianate elements, a five-storey tower, parts of the original hall and a Vanbrughian stable-block clock-tower. The glass-domed winter garden was demolished in 1914 but a loggia survives as the tearoom. Inside there is opulent furniture in the state rooms.

The splendid gardens were laid out by W. E. Nesfield to include a clipped yew maze, specimen trees, statuary, an aviary and glasshouses. More recent attractions include garden trails, deer and a narrow-gauge railway. Just outside the gates, ranged around a picturesque green, stands a Victorian village of thatched cottages built in mock-Tudor style.

Theatre Royal, Westgate Street, Bury St Edmunds IP33 1QR. Telephone: 01284 755127. National Trust.
Open daily except Sundays and bank holidays.

This rare survival of a late Georgian playhouse, built in 1819, was designed by William Wilkins (who also designed the National Gallery, London). It retains a fine pit, boxes and gallery and is a successful working theatre with a national reputation, regularly present-ing drama, opera and dance.

Wingfield Old College and Gardens, Wingfield, Eye IP21 5RA. Telephone: 01379 384888. 4¼ miles (7 km) north-west of Laxfield.
Open Easter to September, weekend afternoons.

The manor house was founded as a college in 1362 by Sir John Wingfield, chief of the Black Prince's council, and retains its great hall from that era. Wingfield Old College is an important, enjoyable and atmospheric timbered building linked with one of the most powerful families in medieval England, the de la Poles. About 1760 a symmetrical classical façade of painted plaster was applied, concealing from outside the old timber frame, which is quite apparent within.

It is now home to Wingfield Arts and Music and is used for exhibitions and concerts. There is a permanent collection of textiles, painting, sculpture and furniture, and 3 acres (1.2 hectares) of gardens with moats and topiary.

Wyken Hall Gardens and Vineyards, Stanton. See page 121.

8
Museums and art galleries

Aldeburgh

Moot Hall Museum, Market Cross Place, Aldeburgh IP15 5DS. Telephone: 01728 452871.
Open May to September, most days.

This fine small building dating from 1520 sheltered a market in the town centre. Later modifications included brick-nogging the timber frame in 1654 and adding twin 'Jacobean' chimneys two hundred years later. Inside is the former court room and a good museum of local history illustrating Aldeburgh's continuing battle with the sea.

Beccles

Beccles and District Museum, Leman House, Ballygate, Beccles NR34 9ND. Telephone: 01502 712308.
Open April to October, Wednesday, Saturday and Sunday afternoons.

The museum occupies a splendid brick and flint building from 1631, modified in 1762. It displays the local history of printing, wherrying and farm implements along with costumes, civic robes and regalia. There is also local coinage from the seventeenth century such as Beccles farthings.

William Clowes Print Museum, Newgate, Beccles NR34 9QE. Telephone: 01502 712884.
Open only by arrangement from June to August on weekday afternoons.

This museum shows developments in printing since 1800 and the associated machinery, with woodcuts and books. It is very relevant to the town, which still has a printing industry.

Brandon

Brandon Heritage Centre, George Street, Brandon IP27 0BX. Telephone: 01842 813707.
Open most weekends and some Thursdays.

This display of the town's history from neolithic times to the present day includes the recreation of a flint knapper's workshop and details of the local fur and forestry industries.

Bungay

Bungay Museum, Council Office, Broad Street, Bungay NR35 1EW. Telephone: 01986 892548.
Open daily.

This is a museum of local history, shown through a collection of coins, photographs and pictures.

Bury St Edmunds

Bury St Edmunds Abbey Visitor Centre, Samson's Tower, Abbey Precinct, Bury St Edmunds IP33 1RS. Telephone: 01284 763110.
Open: April to October, daily; November to March, Wednesdays, Saturdays and Sunday afternoons.

An interpretation of the abbey, with models and commentary, is attractively housed in the modified ruins of the abbey's west front beside a statue of St Edmund by Dame Elizabeth Frink. Samson was the abbot chosen to travel abroad with the ransom money to free the imprisoned Richard Lionheart.

Bury St Edmunds Art Gallery, The Market Cross, Bury St Edmunds IP33 1BT. Telephone: 01284 762081.
Open daily except Sundays and Mondays.

This Market Cross building was designed in 1780 by Robert Adam as a theatre. It is now a venue for a succession of exhibitions and workshops for schools and the general public. The gallery shop sells prints, jewellery, glass and ceramics.

Manor House Museum, Honey Hill, Bury St Edmunds IP33 1HF. Telephone: 01284 757076.
Open daily (closed Sunday mornings).

The museum is a Georgian mansion which has been restored to its eighteenth-century glory. The collections of horology, fine and decorative art and textiles are displayed in superb surroundings and interpreted through computer screens. There is a changing exhibitions programme.

Moyse's Hall Museum, Cornhill, Bury St Edmunds IP33 1DX. Telephone: 01284 757488.
Open daily (closed Sunday mornings).
The collections are housed in one of England's rare surviving Norman houses where some original features are still clearly visible despite the drastic restoration of 1858. In its long history Moyse's Hall has been used as a jail, fire station and railway parcels office before opening as a museum in 1899. The nationally important archaeological collections and local history artefacts are complemented by a lively programme of changing exhibitions.

Suffolk Regiment Museum, The Keep, Gibraltar Barracks, Out Risbygate, Bury St Edmunds IP33 3RN. Telephone: 01284 752394.
Open weekdays.
This prominent crenellated Victorian building displays uniforms, medals and the history of the Suffolk Regiment, which originated as the XIIth Regiment of Foot in 1685 and ceased to exist in 1959, when it amalgamated with the Royal Norfolk Regiment.

Cavendish
Sue Ryder Foundation Museum, Cavendish, Sudbury CO10 8AY. Telephone: 01787 280252.
Open daily.
Sheltered behind a pollarded frontage to the picturesque main street, this museum displays wartime memorabilia and explains the history of the Foundation and the story of Sue Ryder.

Cotton
Mechanical Music Museum Trust, Blacksmith Road, Cotton, Stowmarket IP14 4QN. Telephone: 01449 613876. 5 miles (8 km)

Samson's Tower at Bury St Edmunds is now a visitor centre. The statue of St Edmund is by Dame Elizabeth Frink.

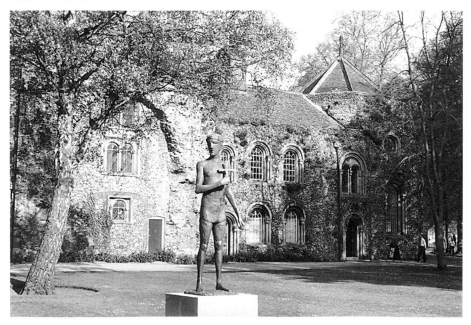

Some of the instruments at the Cotton Mechanical Music Museum.

north of Stowmarket, off B1113.
Open June to September, Sunday afternoons.
Private tours by arrangement during the week.

This fascinating collection comprises reed organs, barrel organs, theatre organs, fairground organs, a huge café organ, street pianos, musical boxes, pianolas, polyphons, organettes and the Wurlitzer theatre pipe organ.

Dunwich

Dunwich Museum, St James Street, Dunwich, Saxmundham IP17 3EA. Telephone: 01728 648796.
Open: Good Friday to October, daily; also weekends in March.

In this museum of natural and local history from Roman times onwards is an interesting model of the medieval town before it was engulfed by the sea.

Felixstowe

Felixstowe Museum, Landguard Fort, Felixstowe IP11 8TW. Telephone: 01394

286403.
Open May to September, Wednesday and Sunday afternoons; also Thursday afternoons in school holidays.

The museum is housed in the ravelin block annexe of the fort (page 76), which is gradually being restored. On display are historical maps, documents, models and artefacts.

Flixton

Norfolk and Suffolk Aviation Museum, The Street, Flixton, Bungay NR35 1NZ. Telephone: 01502 562944. 1³/₄ miles (3 km) southwest of Bungay, on B1062.
Open April to October, Sundays and bank holidays; also Tuesday to Thursday during school summer holidays.

The museum houses a unique collection of memorabilia from the First World War to the present day. Also here are the memorial and museum of the 446th Bomb Group, together with the Royal Observer Corps Museum. Military history is represented by missiles such as the Bloodhound and twenty-four historic aircraft.

Framlingham

Lanman Museum, Framlingham Castle, Framlingham IP13 3BP. Telephone: 01728 723214. English Heritage.
Open Easter to September, daily except Sundays and Mondays.

Local history, paintings and domestic bygones are displayed in an historic setting associated with the castle (page 76).

Halesworth

Halesworth and District Museum, Steeple End, Halesworth IP19 8LL. Telephone contact: 01986 873030.
Open May to September, Wednesdays, Saturdays and Sundays.

The museum, library and art gallery are all housed in the Dutch gabled former Cary Almshouses, which were built in 1686. There are displays of local history, including geology, fossil finds, farming and aspects of rural life. The most important exhibits are archaeological finds from fieldwork and recent excavations conducted by the museum in Halesworth.

Ipswich

Christchurch Mansion and Wolsey Art Gallery, Christchurch Park, Ipswich IP4 2BE. Telephone: 01473 253246.
Open daily except Mondays.

Surrounded by a popular park with arboretum and gardens, Christchurch Mansion was rebuilt in 1548-50 in diaper brickwork to an E plan by Sir Edmund Withipoll on the site of an Augustinian priory. Dutch gables and a porch were added in 1675 to give the present character. It was sold in 1735 and presented to Ipswich in 1895. The mansion is now a museum displaying historic furniture and fine art, including paintings by Constable and Gainsborough, clocks and English porcelain, with eighteenth-century Lowestoft ware.

Ipswich Museum and Exhibition Gallery, High Street, Ipswich IP1 3QH. Telephone: 01473 213761.
Open Tuesday to Saturday.

This is a very comprehensive display of ethnography, archaeology (including good

The Norfolk and Suffolk Aviation Museum at Flixton.

sections on Roman Suffolk) and natural history, featuring British birds, a Victorian natural history gallery and the Suffolk Wildlife Gallery, with a life-size reconstruction of a woolly mammoth. There is a separate exhibition gallery. The building dates from 1880, with an ornate terracotta façade.

Ipswich Transport Museum, Old Trolleybus Depot, Cobham Road, Ipswich IP3 9JD. Telephone: 01473 715666.
Open April to October, Sundays and bank holiday Mondays.
  The museum comprises a collection of over one hundred transport exhibits from the Ipswich area, including cycles, fire engines, delivery vehicles, cranes, buses and trolleybuses.

Lavenham

Guildhall of Corpus Christi, Market Place, Lavenham, Sudbury CO10 9QZ. Telephone: 01787 247646. National Trust.
Open late March to early November, daily, but closed Good Friday.
  This splendid close-studded timber-framed building of 1529 was built as a guildhall but became redundant less than thirty years later. It dominates the Market Place and has seen use as a prison, school and workhouse. In 1950 it was given to the National Trust and now displays a comprehensive exhibition about Suffolk's wool, cloth and horsehair industries. There is also a walled garden with dyers' herbs, a lock-up and a mortuary.

Laxfield

Laxfield and District Museum, The Guildhall, High Street, Laxfield, Woodbridge IP13 8DU. Telephone: 01986 798421.
Open May to September, weekend afternoons and bank holidays.
  Opposite the church, this former sixteenth-century guildhall houses a varied collection recording many aspects of Suffolk village life during the nineteenth and early twentieth centuries, including a reconstructed kitchen, village shop, carpenter's workshop and local photographs. It also has archaeology and natural history displays.

Leiston

The Long Shop Museum, Main Street, Leiston IP16 4ES. Telephone: 01728 832189.
Open April to October, daily.
  The Long Shop Museum is an award-winning steam, industrial and local history museum, housed in part of the original Garrett works site in Leiston. The Long Shop itself is a Grade II* listed building. Completed in 1853, it is an example of one of the earliest assembly line halls in the world. The museum has a number of working steam engines, which are quite often in steam, two early horse-drawn fire-engines, a threshing machine and a living van. There are smaller items relating to Garrett's and the surrounding area.

Lowestoft

East Anglia Transport Museum, Chapel Road, Carlton Colville, Lowestoft NR33 8BL. 3 miles (5 km) south-west of Lowestoft, off B1384. Telephone: 01502 518459.
Open: May to October, Sundays; also Saturdays and some weekdays from June to September.
  Working trams and trolley-buses from five countries are exhibited in a reconstructed 1930s street scene, with a woodland tramline out to Hedley Grove. Other exhibits include cars, steam vehicles and a narrow-gauge railway.

Lowestoft and East Suffolk Maritime Museum, Sparrows Nest, Whapload Road, Lowestoft NR32 1XG. Telephone: 01502 561963.
Open May to September, daily.
  This museum of the fishing industry includes fishing gear, shipwrights' tools and a variety of models.

Lowestoft Museum, Broad House, Nicholas Everitt Park, Oulton Broad, Lowestoft NR33 9JR. Telephone: 01502 511457 or (curator) 572811.
Open April to September, most days.
  The museum features Lowestoft porcelain, geology, archaeology and the history of the area, with a room of domestic bygones.

Royal Naval Patrol Service Association Museum, Europa Room, Sparrows Nest,

The National Horseracing Museum at Newmarket.

Lowestoft NR32 1XG. Telephone: 01502 586250.
Open mid May to mid October, weekdays and Sunday afternoons.

The museum contains a collection of models and uniforms with varied naval documents. There is access to the war memorial.

Mildenhall

Mildenhall and District Museum, 6 King Street, Mildenhall, Bury St Edmunds IP28 7EY. Telephone: 01638 716970.
Open March to Christmas, Wednesdays to Sundays.

This collection of local archaeology and history includes displays about the Mildenhall Treasure (page 70), the local RAF base and the wildlife of Fenland and Breckland.

Newmarket

National Horseracing Museum, 99 High Street, Newmarket CB8 8JL. Telephone: 01638 667333.
Open April to December, daily except Sundays and Mondays.

Four hundred years of racing history are illustrated in art, memorabilia, trophies and graphic displays. Video and computer information is accessible at the touch of a button. It is possible to book in advance for access to the gallops, racing yards and studs.

Palace House Mansion, Palace Street, Newmarket.
Opening 1997.

Charles II's mansion of 1670 was built with several wings with pavilions containing state apartments. Much of the building was replaced in 1863 by a Congregational church, now demolished. One original pavilion remains, extended by the Rothschild family. Eight upper rooms are to be restored and the ground floor is to provide a museum and interpretation centre to give a focus for the town. Nearby Palace House Stables, on the site of Charles II's original racing stables, is undergoing restoration, after which it will provide a live exhibition devoted to racehorse training.

Orford

Dunwich Underwater Exploration Exhibition, Front Street, Orford, Woodbridge IP12 2LW. Telephone: 01394 450678.

Open all year, daily.

This local display of marine archaeology, coastal maps and finds includes an 11 feet (3.4 metres) long bronze cannon recovered from a wreck near the former city of Dunwich.

Parham

390th Bomb Group Memorial Air Museum, Parham Airfield, Parham, Woodbridge IP13 9AF. Telephone: 01473 711275. 1³/₄ miles (3 km) south-east of Framlingham, off B1116.

Open March to November, Sundays and bank holiday Mondays; at other times by appointment.

A local aviation history of the Second World War is displayed in a Nissen hut and in the 1942 control tower of a former USAAF 8th Air Force Flying Fortress bomber base. There are aircraft components, combat records, uniforms, paintings and assorted memorabilia. The four squadrons of 390th Bomb Group flew 301 operations from Parham between 1943 and 1945. By 1944 forty-four United States bomber squadrons were based in East Anglia. At Mildenhall operations were combined with the United States' 8th Air Force.

Shotley Gate

HMS Ganges Association Museum, Shotley Point Marina, Shotley Gate. Telephone: 01473 684749.

Open April to October, weekends.

This museum records the HMS *Ganges* training school which from 1905 to 1976

trained many young sailors on its 143 feet (44 metres) high mast, topped with a platform only 11 inches (279 mm) across, on which the 'button boy' was required to salute. In nearby Shotley church monuments commemorate many Dutch and German sailors.

Southwold

Southwold Lifeboat Museum, Gun Hill, Southwold IP18 6HF.

Open May to September, daily.

This small museum is devoted to the Royal National Lifeboat Institution, with particular emphasis on its work in the Southwold area. The lifeboat station itself, beside the river Blyth, is open to the public when manned.

Southwold Museum, Bartholomew Green, Southwold IP18 6HZ. Telephone: 01502 722437.

Open Easter to September, daily.

Local history, geology and memorabilia including charts of the battle of Sole Bay (1672) feature in this museum, with information about the Southwold railway.

Southwold Sailors' Reading Room, East Cliff, Southwold IP18 6EL.

Open daily.

Photographs, books, model boats and memorabilia of the sea associated with retired seamen are on display here.

Stowmarket

Museum of East Anglian Life, Stowmarket IP14 1DL. Telephone: 01449 612229.

Open April to October, daily, except some Mondays.

This 70 acre (28 hectare) site in the Rattlesden valley retains its medieval Abbot's Hall barn, an easily accessible example of a tithe barn, built for the abbot of St Osyth's Priory to store his share of the parishioners' produce. Its impressive timber-framed interior dates in part from the thirteenth century. All around it stand re-erected buildings, including Alton watermill (from Ipswich), Eastbridge windpump (page 117), Grundisburgh's old smithy and Great Moulton's prefabricated dissenters' chapel from the 1890s.

Haystacking at the Museum of East Anglian Life at Stowmarket.

Edgar's Farmhouse (a modern name) is the remainder of a once larger thatched structure. It has been re-erected and is of interest mainly for its timber frame. Dating from the fourteenth century, it comprises a large communal living space below an imposing roof organised around a focal crown-post which ties the timber frame together structurally and visually. There is no chimney; smoke would have escaped from the central hearth through triangular openings in the gable ends.

The Boby Building, an engineering workshop brought from Bury St Edmunds, is a large framed and weatherboarded building from 1870. It formed part of Robert Boby's engineering works, which specialised in providing machinery for malting, milling, winnowing and flax processing, and now houses an extensive display about East Anglia's industrial heritage, of which the building itself is an example.

Surrounding all these buildings are many associated displays, some demonstrating the operation of early agricultural implements for threshing, ploughing, milling and so on.

Sudbury
Gainsborough's House, 46 Gainsborough Street, Sudbury CO10 6EU. Telephone: 01787 372958.
Open daily except Mondays.

This town house was refronted in Georgian rubbed brickwork in 1723, just before the painter Thomas Gainsborough was born. It is now dedicated to his memory, displaying a large collection of his paintings, drawings and prints. Also on display are period furniture and china. There is a walled garden, an exhibition gallery and an open-access print workshop.

Wattisham
Wattisham Airfield Historical Collection, Wattisham Airfield, Stowmarket IP7 7RA. Telephone: 01449 678189. 1³/₄ miles (3 km) north-east of Bildeston, off B1078.
Open April to October, Sunday afternoons 2.30 to 5 pm; at other times by appointment.

This museum charts the history of the airfield from 1939 to the present, covering its period as an RAF and American air base.

Wetheringsett
Mid-Suffolk Light Railway Society Museum, Brockford Station, Wetheringsett, Stowmarket IP14 5PW. Telephone: 01449 766899 (Sundays and bank holidays); 01473 742358 (at other times). Off A140.

Open Easter to September, Sundays and bank holiday Mondays; also Wednesday afternoons in August.

The 'Middy' was an unusual line intended to serve open agricultural Suffolk but it was never completed; the Railway Society aims to make it a working railway once more, using restored vintage coaches. At present there are artefacts and photographic displays in the restored station buildings and a steam engine on view. There is a pleasant walk along part of the route of the railway track which ran here from 1904 to 1952.

Woodbridge

Suffolk Horse Museum, Shire Hall, Market Hill, Woodbridge IP12 4LU. Telephone: 01394 380643.

Open Easter to September, daily.

The Suffolk Punch is a chestnut-coloured heavy working horse first recorded in 1506. All Suffolk Punches alive today are descended from one foaled in 1760 in Ufford. These horses are typically fifteen or sixteen hands high, tremendously strong but gentle-natured, weighing about one tonne. Until the 1940s they did most of the agricultural work and pulled most road transport, but the breed nearly died out in the 1960s. Now they are looked after by the Suffolk Horse Society and this museum includes models, displays, associated social history, paintings from 1790 and photographs, all in the historic setting of the Shire Hall.

Woodbridge Museum, 5 Market Hill, Woodbridge IP12 4LP. Telephone: 01394 380502.

Open April to October, Thursdays to Sundays.

Local archaeology and historic finds from Sutton Hoo and Burrow Hill are exhibited, with profiles of Woodbridge characters. These include Thomas Seckford (page 53) and Edward Fitzgerald (1809-83), known for his free translation (popularised by Dante Gabriel Rossetti and Tennyson) of Omar Khayyam's eleventh-century philosophical *Rubaiyat*. Woodbridge was also home to the lawyer and artist Thomas Churchyard (1798-1865) and Isaac Johnson (1754-1835), surveyor and mapmaker.

Woolpit

Woolpit and District Museum, The Institute, Village Centre, Woolpit IP30 9RF. Telephone: 01359 240822.

Open Easter to end of September, Saturday, Sunday and bank holiday afternoons.

This small museum depicts life in a Suffolk village. There is a permanent display on Woolpit brickmaking. Other displays are changed annually.

9
Industry and transport

From early times Suffolk established links with foreign lands: Saxon traders linked east Suffolk to towns on the river Rhine and medieval Ipswich traded with the Hanseatic League. Suffolk's most significant industry, the weaving of woollen cloth, flourished through the fifteenth and sixteenth centuries, but it declined as the industrial revolution gathered pace and cloth manufacture moved north. Suffolk was left to concentrate on agriculture, which eventually brought back prosperity. Vanished industries have left names like Coprolite Street, Leatherbottle Hill, Rope Walk and Weavers Row.

The cloth and textile industries included spinning and the manufacture of sailcloth, sackcloth, broadcloth and linen, with early wool-based products later giving way to those made from hemp and flax and subsequent later diversification. Many of the old cloth towns, bypassed by the industrial revolution, have matured into picturesque villages.

The old draperies

In 1326 King Edward III offered franchises to fullers, weavers and dyers, thereby attracting to East Anglia Flemish clothworkers fleeing the Hundred Years War.

The early cloth centres of Bury St Edmunds, Ipswich and Sudbury were augmented by Long Melford, Lavenham, Hadleigh, Clare and Kersey; all produced strong heavy broadcloths with local variations. Thus arose the coarse blue 'Kerseymere' (for horsemen's cloaks), 'Gleynforth' from Glemsford, 'Linsey Wolseys' and thick-twilled fustians from Haverhill. Colours varied from puce (blue black) to popinjay green; red hues came from madder. Quantities of wool and cloth were exported via London to Russia and Spain. Increasing demand caused quality to improve, refined by standards such as the 1468 statute requiring East Anglian broad-

cloths to weigh 38 pounds (17 kg) and measure 28½ yards (26 metres) by 1¾ yards (1.6 metres).

Until the spinning wheel was invented in 1530 wool was laboriously spun using a spindle and a distaff, a cleft stick 3 feet (90 cm) long. After weaving, the cloth was beaten, maybe by a watermill-driven mechanical hammer, before scrubbing, degreasing, scouring and dyeing. Around 1450-1530 the cloth industry peaked in the triangle of Clare, Bury St Edmunds and East Bergholt, Suffolk was producing more than any other English county, importing wool from surrounding counties. Thus a range of associated trades – carders, spinners, weavers, dyers, fullers and shearers – was co-ordinated by wealthy clothiers who bought the wool, organised the processing and marketed the final product. They also built fine houses and churches, for example at Lavenham and Long Melford, but their fortunes declined through recession in the sixteenth century, provoking civil disobedience which reflected wars at home and in Europe and a changing market.

The new draperies

During the reign of Elizabeth I heavy broadcloths went out of fashion. In came lighter, more colourful fabrics like grosgrains, velures, mockadoes, bays ('baize'), silks, satins and velvets. Many Suffolk towns failed to adapt and stagnated, becoming merely yarn suppliers to weavers in Norwich and Essex. A few centres diversified, like Sudbury (silk, crepe and flags) and Bungay (knitted worsted stockings). Lace was associated with Eye and Needham Market, blankets with Bildeston.

New techniques from Lombardy were introduced by Dutch refugees who congregated in towns like Norwich and Colchester, unlike earlier Flemish settlers who preferred the country. At the same time industrial technology began to replace cottage industry: the spinning jenny and flying shuttle required more power, so the cloth industry moved north to stronger rivers and steam power.

Hemp

Hemp was grown from the sixteenth century to the nineteenth, especially between Lopham and Beccles, leaving place-names like Heckfield Green and Bleach Green. Hemp resembles a nettle and flourished in lush river valleys, often supplementing income from cattle grazing. To make cloth, the hemp stem was pulled, retted in water, beaten with a hinged bar and then heckled or separated out with a rough iron comb. The result was spun or woven into smocks, sheets, bolsters, bed ticking, sackcloth, sailcloth, rope and fishing nets.

Flax

A flax-based linen industry grew in the seventeenth century, becoming increasingly popular because of the softness of the cloth. Operations were centred on Hoxne, Witnesham, Long Melford and the valleys of the Waveney and Little Ouse.

Other textiles in the nineteenth century

Straw from Victorian cornfields supported a straw-plaiting industry, producing, for example, straw hats in south-west Suffolk. The wetter osier beds supplied raw material for basketmaking and wickerwork, now a rural craft. Skills in textiles led to the development of other factories to weave coconut fibre into ropes and matting. There were ten such factories in Glemsford alone, which in 1906 produced a coir carpet for Olympia measuring 63,000 square feet (5853 square metres). The industry survived, almost entirely in Babergh district, until the 1930s.

Horsehair weaving peaked from 1830 to 1870, when raw material was imported from Siberia and South America to be turned into mattresses, crinoline, brushes, blinds and the seating in liners and railway carriages. There were factories in Hadleigh, Haverhill, Long Melford and Glemsford and the last to be built was at Lavenham in 1908. This industry, too, survived until the 1930s.

Spiralling costs of silk production in London and local cheap adaptable labour encouraged relocation of this industry from Spitalfields to Glemsford in 1824. There were several factories in Sudbury by the 1830s, with six hundred looms operating at the peak, utilising raw silk from China and Japan. Sudbury retained its expertise, producing for example the Coronation dress worn by Queen Elizabeth II.

Watermills and windmills

Watermills grinding corn in the county are recorded at Domesday. In the later middle ages they powered the cloth industry and later still spun silk. By the 1850s around a hundred were left, three powered by the tide but most taking energy from a millpond, using water under or over a millwheel. Many of these mills are weatherboarded, often with an adjacent miller's house.

A windmill was recorded at Bury St Edmunds in 1191 and in 1830 William Cobbett saw seventeen from a single viewpoint in Ipswich: 'they are all painted and washed white; the sails are black; it was a fine morning, the wind was brisk, and their twirling all together added greatly to the beauty of the scene.' Poor roads encouraged every village to have its own windmill, even though the work was dusty and dangerous. Sails powered millstones, operated hoists and sometimes pumped water. By 1880 there were over four hundred windmills in Suffolk; the swift decline thereafter reflected improvements in steam power and road transport; only thirteen still worked in 1939.

Windmills are of three types. Post mills are the earliest and most common, with sails carried on a weatherboarded body supported by a massive central post encased in a brick roundhouse. The post is pivoted, allowing the sails to be turned into the wind, often by means of a fantail. After 1800 there were more durable and powerful tower mills of tapering masonry, rising five storeys or more, surmounted by a revolving cap carrying the sails and fantail. Smaller timber-framed structures are termed smock mills, cheap to build but short-lived.

Huge maltings in Ipswich docks are being converted to other uses.

A number of watermills and windmills are regularly open to the public.

Fishing

Medieval coastal towns combined sea fishing with maritime trade as far afield as the Faeroes and Iceland. The rewards were good and fishing provided enormous quantities of herrings with which coastal towns paid their tithes.

Medieval ports silted up, restricting trade, but fishermen continued to make a living, despite competition and piracy. They concentrated on plaice and sole in summer, on sprats, herring and cod in winter. Mackerel, lobster, oysters and eels were also caught.

By the early twentieth century the Lowestoft and Great Yarmouth area was a fishing centre of great importance. There, in 1913, nearly two thousand herring drifters landed ninety million fish, having sailed to Ireland, Shetland and the west coast of Scotland. As the boats journeyed south, hundreds of shore girls followed, gutting and packing catches, which began to decline around 1920.

Today fishing industry quotas affect both deeper-sea vessels (mostly based at Lowestoft) and longshoremen from Dunwich or Aldeburgh who work from tarred timber huts with chalk boards displaying the morning's catch, selling it from the beach. Below their winches and drying nets are their colourful beach-launched open-topped clinker boats.

Sea angling is popular, especially for whiting and cod in the colder months; eels, flat fish and bass are also taken.

Shipbuilding and sailing

Early foreign trade and local oak woods stimulated shipbuilding, which reached a peak in Tudor times, providing ships against the Spanish Armada. Thereafter Ipswich remained important but larger ships tended to be built in deeper ports. However, wherries and sailing barges, especially Thames barges with their graceful broad lines, were built in places like Pin Mill. They were ideal for the east coast, their flat bottoms easing them over mudflats and sandbars and up shallow creeks. Lee boards were lowered each side instead of a keel and huge sails were supported on a diagonal spar, the sprit, which was a many-winched rig easily operated by a man and boy, important for easy handling and negotiating bridges.

A sailors' landmark (not open to the public) is the tall pointed tower of the Royal Hospital School for Sailors' Sons at Holbrook, founded at Greenwich in 1715 but moved to Suffolk in 1933.

Boatbuilding and the yachting industry now provide employment in many Suffolk coastal towns.

Navigations

Trade from coastal ports was at one time carried inland by converting rivers into navigations with locks, wharves and towpaths. Thus sailing wherries and horse-drawn and steam-powered barges were able to transform towns like Halesworth and Sudbury, bringing corn, malt, tar, tallow, osiers, coal, slate, timber, lime, flour, guncotton and chemicals. The most famous navigation was the Stour: its locks and barges were often painted by Constable. Navigations were initiated by Act of Parliament, granted on the Stour in 1705, on the Blyth in 1757, on the Waveney about 1760, on the Gipping in 1790, on the Lark in the late nineteenth century. Most navigations were disused by 1939, overtaken by railways.

Malting

In the middle ages most towns had maltings and pubs made their own beer. Industrial development was restrained by taxes on malt, yet Patrick Stead of Halesworth pioneered a mechanised process which, when the tax dropped, enabled trade to expand rapidly. Many new maltings were erected, encouraged by navigations and railways which linked them to breweries in London and Burton upon Trent. They were often immense three-storey build-ings, of massive brickwork with internal iron frames and characteristic ventilators on the roof. Many are now redundant.

Typically, barley was stored until winter, then soaked in water and spread out on the malting floors to germinate, being regularly turned and finally returned to the kilns to be dried and stored. In 1844 there were 110 maltings (with kiln roofs); by 1900 this figure had dropped to sixty-five. In the twentieth century the industry has grown fast and by the 1970s the biggest names were Adnams (Southwold), Greene King (Bury St Edmunds) and Tolly Cobbold (Ipswich). They have since been joined by smaller companies including Mauldons, Forbes, Scotties and Green Dragon.

Maltings converted for the arts can be visited at Snape (page 46) and at the Quay Theatre, Sudbury. A number of large maltings remain in Ipswich docks, and there is also the Malt Kiln pub on Wherry Quay.

Engineering and railways

Agricultural needs drove engineering in Suffolk and Victorian factories prospered. Famous firms included Whitmore & Binyon of Wickham Market (steam engines) and Garretts of Leiston (page 30). Smythes of Peasenhall were famous for a particularly effective seed-drill. Ransomes of Ipswich were founded in 1789, patenting their cast-iron ploughshare in 1803 and expanding rapidly in the 1830s after the arrival of the railway, with a lawn-mower (in 1832) and then a self-moving steam engine. In 1844 the YL plough led to a world-famous steam plough. Much later Ransomes produced the first petrol-driven lawn-mower.

Power generation

Abundant opportunities for solar, wind and wave power have not yet been utilised, though there are two nuclear power stations at Sizewell.

Bardwell Windmill, Bardwell, Bury St Edmunds (OS 144, 155: TL 941738). Telephone: 01359 251331. 2^1/2 miles (4 km) north of Ixworth off A143.
Open daily except Saturdays and Mondays.

A tower mill with four sails and a beehive cap, Bardwell Mill was built in 1823 and worked until 1925, when an oil engine was installed. It was restored in the mid 1980s but the sails were torn off in the 1987 gale.

Boat World, Sea Lake Road, Oulton Broad, Lowestoft NR32 3LQ. Telephone: 01502 500661. ^{1}/2 mile (1 km) west of Lowestoft.

Winding warp yarn from stein to bobbin at Gainsborough Silk Weaving Company.

Open May to September, Monday to Friday.

This training college for boatbuilders has become a centre of excellence for traditional timber boatbuilding. Visitors can watch work in progress on a variety of craft in workshops beside Lake Lothing.

Buttrum's Mill, Burkitt Road, Woodbridge (OS 169: TM 264493). Telephone: 01473 265162.

Open May to September, Saturday and Sunday afternoons.

This six-storey tower windmill, built in 1836, retains intact machinery including four pairs of millstones. It worked commercially until 1928 and, now restored, its four shuttered sails and fantail still run regularly. There is a small exhibition on the ground floor.

Framsden Windmill, Framsden, Stowmarket IP14 6HB (OS 156: TM 192598). Telephone: 01473 890328. 2$^1/_2$ miles (4 km) south-east of Debenham off B1077.

Open at weekends by appointment.

A large post mill with a two-storey roundhouse was first built here in 1760 and modified in 1836. It worked until 1934 and was renovated from 1966 to 1973.

Gainsborough Silk Weaving Company, Alexandra Road, Sudbury CO10 6XH. Telephone: 01787 372081.

Open by appointment.

Frequent tours are available of this working factory, including its looms and dye house. There is also a small museum with historic artefacts, including some of the earliest powered Jacquard looms, and a history of the company over the past century.

George E. Cook, Basketmaker, Friday Street Farm, Farnham, Saxmundham IP17 1JX. Telephone: 01728 603309. 2$^1/_2$ miles (4 km) north-west of Snape, off A1094.

Open April to October, daily.

Visitors to this workshop can see a range of traditional baskets being made by hand

and rush and cane seats being repaired.

Greene King Brewery, Westgate Brewery, Westgate Street, Bury St Edmunds IP33 1QT. Telephone: 01284 763222.
During the summer tours can be booked by telephone through the Bury St Edmunds tourist information centre (01284 764667).

The brewery was founded in 1799 and is famous for its real ale brands, particularly Abbot Ale. It occupies imposing buildings close to the town centre. The pavement copper is a distinctive landmark.

Herringfleet Windpump, Herringfleet, Lowestoft (OS 134: TM 466976). Telephone: 01473 265162. 4¼ miles (7 km) north-west of Lowestoft off B1074.
Open occasionally – locally advertised.

This three-storey tarred weatherboarded smock drainage mill was built in 1820 and is accessible only by public footpath from the B1074. It features cloth-spread sails and a boat-shaped cap turned manually by a tailpole and winch. Water was lifted from drainage ditch to embanked river by an encased 16 feet (4.9 metres) diameter external scoopwheel. A survivor of the old-style Broadland windpumps, it worked regularly until the 1950s. The marshman was provided with a fireplace.

Holton Windmill, Holton, Halesworth IP19 8PW (OS 156: TM 403774). Telephone: 01986 872367. 1¼ miles (2 km) east of Halesworth, off B1123.
Open Spring bank holiday Monday and Late Summer bank holiday; at other times by appointment.

This small mid eighteenth-century post mill has a white timber body above a tarred brick roundhouse and worked until about 1900.

Letheringham Watermill, Letheringham, Woodbridge IP13 7RE. Telephone: 01728 746349. 2 miles (3 km) north-west of Wickham Market, off B1078.
Open March to May and July to August, Sundays and bank holiday Mondays.

This picturesque weatherboarded mill, set

Herringfleet Windpump, with water-meadows and drainage ditch in the background.

in 5 acres (2 hectares) of delightful gardens with a riverside walk, stopped work before the Second World War. Most of the machinery was removed, but a new wooden waterwheel has been constructed and can be seen turning.

The Long Shop Museum, Main Street, Leiston IP16 4ES. See page 106.

Lowestoft fish market and harbour area. Telephone: 01502 523004.
Guided tours, mornings only.

Visitors get a general view over the working boats and their catch although access is no longer possible to the ice factory or on board trawlers.

Lydia Eva and ***Mincarlo***, Lowestoft Harbour (yacht basin by bascule bridge). Telephone: 01502 565234.
From Easter to October, one of the two vessels will always be in Lowestoft, open daily.

(The other will be at Great Yarmouth and they will swap locations periodically.)

Lydia Eva is the last surviving steam herring drifter of the 1930s era when some three thousand similar vessels supported the East Anglian herring industry. *Mincarlo* is the last remaining side-fishing trawler completely built and engined in Lowestoft from the 1960s era.

Museum of East Anglian Life, Stowmarket IP14 1DL. Telephone. 01449 612229. See also page 108.

Open April to October, daily, except some Mondays.

Alton Watermill and its machinery were moved to the museum from Stutton in 1973-4 when the site was flooded by the creation of Alton Water. A corn mill of eighteenth-century origin, it worked until the 1960s, its overshot wheel driving three pairs of stones.

Eastbridge Windpump is a smock mill with fully shuttered sails driving a triple plunger pump. It was built around 1850 at the Minsmere Level and was in use until 1940. It collapsed in 1977 and was rebuilt at the museum in 1979.

Pakenham Watermill, Grimstone End, Pakenham, Bury St Edmunds IP31 2LZ. 6 miles (9 km) north-east of Bury St Edmunds. Telephone: 01787 247179.

Open Easter to September, Wednesday, Saturday, Sunday and bank holiday afternoons.

Mills have stood here since Norman times – there are Tudor remains below the present eighteenth-century building which worked commercially until 1974. In 1978 it was restored by Suffolk Preservation Society and now produces stoneground flour as well as displaying an exhibition. Pakenham also has a large windmill.

Saxtead Green Post Mill, Saxtead Green, Framlingham IP13 9QQ (OS 156. TM 254644). Telephone: 01728 685789. 1¾ miles (3 km) west of Framlingham off A1120. English Heritage.

Open April to September, Monday to Saturday.

A mill was recorded on this site in 1287.

The post mill at Saxtead Green, near Framlingham.

The present elegant white-boarded building dates from 1706 and after extensive nineteenth-century modernisation worked until 1947. It was altered again in the late 1950s and now has a three-storey painted brick roundhouse.

Sizewell Visitor Centre, Nuclear Electric plc, Sizewell B Power Station, near Leiston IP16 4UR. Telephone: 01728 642139. 1³/₄ miles (3 km) east of Leiston.
Open daily.
This is a multi-media exhibition about nuclear power generation and environmental issues. Guided tours of the station are available for pre-booked parties, who can also visit the site of Sizewell A (a first-generation magnox station) and Sizewell B (Britain's first pressurised water reactor).

Stanton Windmill, Upthorpe Road, Stanton, Bury St Edmunds IP31 2AW (OS 144, 155: TL 971733). Telephone: 01359 250622. 2¹/₂ miles (4 km) north-east of Ixworth off A143.
Open at any reasonable time on application to the mill house.
This post mill dating from 1751 was moved to its present site *c*.1820, when it gained a roundhouse. It was restored from 1985 to 1993 and is now in full working order. It has four patent sails, two pairs of stones and a fantail.

Thelnetham Windmill, Mill Road, Thelnetham, near Diss IP22 1JZ (OS 144: TM 011790). Telephone contact: 01473 250622. 5 miles (8 km) north of Walsham le Willows.
Open on Sundays and bank holidays at Easter, in May, then from July to September.
This four-storey black tower mill is fitted with huge patent sails and a conical white cap. Built in 1819, it was modernised in 1832 and worked commercially until 1924. Stoneground flour is still produced.

Thorpeness Post Mill, Thorpeness Mere, Thorpeness (OS 156: TM 468598). Telephone: 01473 265131.

Open Saturday and Sunday afternoons at Easter and from May to September; every afternoon in July and August.
Built in 1803 as a post mill at Aldringham, this mill was moved in 1922 to become a village feature, sited over a well to feed a water tower (the 'House in the Clouds') until 1940. Restored in 1977, it is now a Suffolk Heritage Coast information centre.

Tolly Cobbold Brewery, Cliff Road, Ipswich IP3 0AZ. Telephone: 01473 231723.
Guided tours, May to September, daily at noon, and also by appointment.
This brewery was rebuilt in 1896 above its own holy well. There is a working display with artefacts from 1723 (when Thomas Cobbold founded the brewery), redolent of malt and hops, and reputedly the oldest brewing vessel in the world. A steam engine and the cooperage can also be seen. From the malt mill, mash tun and copper room are produced a range of traditional cask and bottled ales which can be sampled at the Brewery Tap bar on the premises.

Woodbridge Tide Mill, Tide Mill Quay, Woodbridge (OS 169: TM 276487). Telephone: 01473 626618.
Open May to September, daily; also Easter weekend and weekends in October.
A mill stood here in 1170. The present weatherboarded building dates from 1793 and until 1957 drew tidal power from a 7¹/₂ acre (3 hectare) millpond fed by the river Deben. The mill was restored in 1982 with an 18 feet (5.5 metres) diameter wheel fed from a small demonstration pond and is one of the best-known historic buildings in Suffolk. Adjacent is the granary building.

Wrentham Basketware, London Road, Wrentham, Beccles. Telephone: 01502 675628. 5 miles (8 km) north of Southwold, off A12.
Open daily.
This English willow basketmaking workshop produces many designs in traditional styles.

10
Agriculture

Suffolk's huge barns, the longest reaching 180 feet (55 metres), recall agricultural prosperity dating back to the thirteenth century. The larger examples, built from aisled timber frames or in massive brickwork ventilated by slit windows, normally had a cart entry and space for the threshing and storage of grain.

By the sixteenth century the county's agricultural expertise contrasted with a general economic slump as much of the cloth industry moved away from the area, leaving un employment and increasing poverty.

During this period Suffolk became well-known for its dairy farming; though the butter was delicious and gave rise to many buttermarkets, the cheese was apparently of poor quality. Through the seventeenth and eighteenth centuries, Red Poll cattle were bred in the north of the county. Hornless, with white udders and tails, they were good milkers and fattened well in poor pasture. Also popular were British White cattle, which had historically been kept in parks by the religious orders (along with deer). Beef cattle enjoyed grazing Suffolk's water-meadows, many being brought to the area from as far afield as Scotland by drovers. In the early eighteenth century, Daniel Defoe noted more than three hundred annual droves in Suffolk, each of up to one thousand animals.

Lush pastureland was good for grazing cattle, and Suffolk's oak forests provided the oak bark which was essential (with lime) for tanning cattle skins into leather. Thus a leather industry developed, especially from 1780 to 1850, producing goods ranging from shoes to drive belts for the new agricultural machines. Leather products were made in many Suffolk towns for local use or exported as far as India and Russia.

Other farm animals having close historical associations with Suffolk are Suffolk Punch heavy horses (page 110) and Suffolk sheep.

Sheep had been kept in the county for centuries but their numbers increased as root crops were more commonly used as winter feed. From the early nineteenth century onwards Norfolk horned ewes were crossed with Southdown rams to produce 'blackfaces', officially recognised as Suffolks in 1859. From the 1880s they were bred more for mutton than wool and in 1886 the Suffolk Sheep Society was founded. These sheep are now found all over the world.

The threat of Napoleonic invasion, possibly through Suffolk, brought troops into the county and thereby boosted demand for local corn, and also for rabbits, which were kept in warrens (see page 13). When peace with France was declared in 1815, Suffolk's corn prices plummeted, bringing poverty; it has been suggested that at this time some 30 per cent of the county's working population was unemployed.

For centuries various Corn Laws had been in place in England; by restricting the import and export of grain, they had kept its price artificially high. In 1846 the Corn Laws were repealed, allowing a free market, which stimulated agriculture and thereby industrial development. Corn exchanges were built in many towns, boosting the economy and leading to Suffolk's labour-intensive high farming period of 1850-80. The railways arrived in Suffolk at this time; there was steam power in the fields and a host of engineering firms concentrated on making agricultural products. This ideal situation did not last, as cheap American grain began to be imported in the 1880s and increasing mechanisation led to redundancy both of labourers in the fields and of windmills to grind flour.

Some of the changes to the landscape wrought by new agricultural practices since 1900 have already been described, bringing such crops as rape and linseed to fields that used to grow wheat and barley. Amongst the most successful newer crops has been sugar beet, grown in quantity since 1920. Government subsidies and the wartime rationing of sugar cane encouraged it and the crop thrives in central Suffolk's heavy clay soil. It is locally processed.

Vines were planted by the Romans and by 1086 more than 40 per cent of Britain's recorded vineyards, often associated with priories, were in East Anglia, especially the Stour valley. In recent decades winemaking has again become popular, producing fresh, very dry white wines from vines such as Muller Thurgau and Bacchus.

Abundant local apples are crushed to produce a range of juices or fermented in oak barrels for cider, which, years ago, was used to pay tithes. Eating apples are also grown, especially Cox and Russet.

The Suffolk Show takes place every May at Suffolk Showground, Bucklesham Road, Ipswich IP3 8UH. Telephone: 01473 726847.

Baylham House Rare Breeds Farm, Mill Lane, Baylham, Ipswich. Telephone: 01473 830264.
Open April to September, Tuesday to Sunday.

This is a collection of breeding groups of cattle, pigs, sheep, goats and poultry with a paddock where children can feed them.

Boyton Vineyard, Stoke by Clare, Sudbury CO10 8TB. Telephone: 01440 61893.
Open April to October, daily.

This vineyard was planted in 1977 and tours, talks and tastings are available. The medieval farmhouse and its gardens are also of interest.

Bruisyard Wines, Church Road, Bruisyard, Saxmundham IP17 2EF. Telephone: 01728 638281. West of Saxmundham, off A12.
Open mid January to Christmas, daily.

This 10 acre (4 hectare) vineyard with its own winery is supplemented by ornamental herb and water gardens and a wooded picnic area.

Cavendish Manor Vineyard, Nether Hall, Cavendish, Sudbury CO10 8BX. Telephone: 01787 280221.
Open daily.

This picturesque vineyard is planted beside a fifteenth-century manor house and also offers a small museum and arboretum.

Copella Fruit Juices Ltd, Hill Farm, Boxford, Sudbury CO10 5NY. Telephone: 01787 210496.
Open daily.

Visitors can sample the farm-pressed sparkling and fresh fruit juices produced here.

Cow Wise, Meadow Farm, West Stow, Bury St Edmunds IP28 6EZ. Telephone: 01284 728862. $3^3/4$ miles (6 km) north-west of Bury St Edmunds.
Open April to August, bank holiday Sundays and Mondays.

This working dairy farm concentrates on Friesian and Jersey cows, which visitors can watch being milked from a special gallery. There are also calves, hens, goats and lambs and wildlife displays.

Easton Farm Park, Easton, near Wickham Market IP13 0EQ. Telephone: 01728 746475.
Open mid March to end of September, daily.

The park includes farm buildings on the Duke of Hamilton's estate, with a working smithy, vintage farm machinery and a collection of farm animals, including some rare breeds and Suffolk horses. The Victorian dairy is particularly splendid.

Gifford's Hall Vineyard, Hartest, Bury St Edmunds. Telephone: 01284 830464. $7^1/2$ miles (12 km) south of Bury St Edmunds, off B1066.
Open Easter to October, daily.

Since 1986 Gifford's Hall has been managed as a country living. There are 14 acres (5.7 hectares) of vines with a winery, and a rose garden, apiary, flower garden, wildflower meadow and a selection of farm animals, many of rare breeds.

James White's Apple Juice and Cider Company, White's Fruit Farm, Helmingham Road, Ashbocking, Ipswich IP6 9JS. Telephone: 01473 890111. $6^1/4$ miles (10 km)

north of Ipswich, off B1077.
Open daily (but only the farm shop is open at weekends).

Visitors are welcome to sample the products and watch cider pressing, which takes place from October to February.

Kentwell Hall Home Farm, Long Melford, Sudbury CO10 9BA. Telephone: 01787 310207. (For Kentwell Hall see page 99).
Open usually daily in the afternoon.

Rare breeds are kept amongst old timbered buildings including a fourteenth-century barn, a cow byre and a shippon.

Otley College of Agriculture and Horticulture, Otley, Ipswich IP6 9EY. Telephone: 01473 785543.
Open days in April and September, advertised locally.

The college welcomes visitors on open days to see its dairy unit and exhibitions of its work.

Pentlow Farm, The Children's Farm, Cavendish, Sudbury. Telephone: 01787 280194.
Open March to August, Sundays; also weekday afternoons in school holidays.

The Children's Farm is organised so that children are able safely to meet British farm animals, especially baby animals whenever they are there, and watch them being fed.

Rede Hall Farm Park, Rede, Bury St Edmunds IP29 4UG. Telephone: 01284 850695. 6 miles (9 km) south-west of Bury St Edmunds, off A143.
Open April to September, daily.

This working farm is based on the agricultural life lived from 1930 to 1950. Thus traditional Suffolk horses draw carts and wagons and are shod by the working farrier. Farm implements, seasonal activities and management techniques relate to the same period. There is also a nature trail.

Shawsgate Vineyard, Badingham Road, Framlingham IP13 8HZ. Telephone: 01728 724060.
Open April to October, daily.

This 17 acre (6.9 hectare) vineyard has a modern stainless steel winery. There are guided tours and tastings. Wine and ciders are on sale all year.

Wyken Hall Gardens and Vineyards, Wyken Hall, Stanton, Bury St Edmunds IP31 2DW. Telephone: 01359 250287. Follow signs from A143 at Ixworth.
Open February to December, Thursdays, Fridays, Sundays and bank holidays.

This vineyard forms part of an estate around a manor house of Elizabethan origins. There are 4 acres (1.6 hectares) of gardens, including formal and wild gardens, nuttery, maze and old orchard. There is a walk through ancient woodland to the vineyard. Wyken wine is sold in the café and country store located in the old barn.

The Victorian dairy at Easton Farm Park has a splendid tiled interior.

11
Other places to visit

British Birds of Prey and Conservation Centre, Stonham Barns, Pettaugh Road, Stonham Aspal, Stowmarket IP14 6AT. Telephone: 01449 711425. 5 miles (8 km) east of Stowmarket off A1120.
Open daily.

A collection of falcons, kestrels, hawks, eagles, buzzards, kites, hobbies and every species of British owl is displayed in aviaries. There are flying demonstrations. Stonham Barns includes craft shops and galleries.

Corn Craft, Bridge Farm, Monks Eleigh, Ipswich IP7 7AX. Telephone: 01449 740456
Open daily.

Corn Craft produces traditional corn dollies and dried flowers for the gift trade and sells a range of craft products.

East of England Birds of Prey and Conservation Centre, St Jacob's Hall, Laxfield, Woodbridge IP13 8HY. Telephone: 01986 798844. 1¼ miles (2 km) south-east of Laxfield, off B1117.
Open April to October, daily; November to March, weekends only.

A collection of hawks, owls, falcons and eagles is on view in large aviaries. There are daily flying demonstrations by falconers.

Mickfield Fish and Water Garden Centre, Debenham Road, Mickfield, Stowmarket. Telephone: 01449 711336. Off A140.
Open daily.

This working nursery has ornamental water gardens and a wide selection of fish.

The National Stud, Newmarket CB8 0XE. Telephone: 01638 663464. 2½ miles (4 km) south-west of Newmarket, by the July Racecourse.
Open March to August, daily; also September and October race days. Tours by appointment only.

The National Stud was founded during the First World War and it moved to Suffolk in 1963. A working thoroughbred stud where visitors can see stallions, mares and foals, it is probably best visited in the spring.

Netherfield Herb Garden, Nether Street, Rougham, Bury St Edmunds IP30 9LW. Telephone: 01359 270452. 3¾ miles (6 km) south-east of Bury St Edmunds.
Open daily.

The modest garden of this thatched cottage is planted with scores of aromatic herbs, many formally laid out in small box-edged patterns and appropriately labelled.

Orford Ness, Orford. Telephone: 01394 450637 (ferry from Orford). National Trust.
Open April to October, Thursday to Saturday; in winter for only two days each month. Access is only by ferry, which must be booked in advance. Visitor numbers strictly limited.

Military experiments were conducted at Orford Ness, taken by the Experimental Flying Section in 1915 and vacated by the Atomic Weapons Research Establishment in 1971. Concrete pagodas were built in the 1960s to test triggers for nuclear warheads. Later 189 masts, 197 feet (60 metres) high, marked the Cobra Mist intelligence system, reputed to be able to see beyond the horizon; its receiver station was near Bangkok, but the transmitter apparently became redundant only eighteen months after completion.

Visitors follow a 3½ mile (5.6 km) route over the nature reserve (page 67), on vegetated shingle to the lighthouse.

The Otter Trust, Earsham, Bungay NR35 2AF. Telephone: 01986 893470. 1¼ miles (2 km) west of Bungay, on the Norfolk border.
Open April to October, daily.

This is the largest collection of otters in the world. They can be seen in natural enclosures beside the river Waveney, where the British otter is bred for reintroduction to the wild.

Pleasurewood Hills American Theme Park, Lowestoft. Telephone: 01502 508200. North of Lowestoft, off A12.
Open May to September, also parts of April and October, daily.
This is one of Britain's major theme parks, providing abundant rides, shows and attractions (subject to the weather).

Potteries
A range of pots can be seen at Aldringham Craft Market, Aldringham (telephone: 01728 830397), and at other centres such as Snape Maltings Riverside Centre (see page 46) and Stonham Barns, Stonham Aspal (telephone: 01449 711755). There are periodic craft markets at Blackthorpe Barn off the A14 at Rougham (telephone: 01359 270238). Suffolk Craft Society (telephone: 01379 740711) provides a directory of craftspeople working in the county and organises exhibitions each August in the Peter Pears Gallery, Aldeburgh, and in November at Bury St Edmunds Art Gallery. Members' work can also be purchased at Craftco, High Street, Southwold (telephone: 01502 723211). There are a number of working potteries with showrooms open to the public. It is advisable to check opening times before making a visit.
Blythburgh Pottery and Dorothy Midson Ceramics, Chapel Road, Blythburgh, Halesworth IP19 9LW. Telephone: 01502 70234.
Butley Pottery, Mill Lane, Butley, Woodbridge IP12 3PA. Telephone: 01394 450785.
Carter's Tea Pots, Low Road, Debenham, Stowmarket IP14 6QU. Telephone: 01728 860475.
Chediston Pottery, The Duke, Chediston Green, Halesworth IP19 0BB. Telephone: 01986 785242. Open by appointment.
Church Cottage Pottery, Wilby, Eye. Telephone: 01379 384253.
Henry Watson's Potteries Ltd, Wattisfield, Diss IP22 1NH. Telephone: 01359 251239.
JK Pottery, Leiston Road, Knodishall, Saxmundham. Telephone: 01728 832901.
Kersey Pottery, The Street, Kersey, Ipswich.

Telephone: 01473 822092.
Milestone House Pottery, High Street, Yoxford, Saxmundham IP17 3EP. Telephone: 01728 668465.
Bernard Rooke Pottery, Mill Gallery, Swilland, Ipswich. Telephone: 01473 785460.

RAF Lakenheath, Lakenheath, Brandon. Telephone: 01638 522151. Just west of Lakenheath, off A1065.
Open for guided tours of the base to pre-booked groups of ten to forty persons only.
An exhibition illustrates the history of this extensive military base and its links with the United States Air Force. Visitors can watch F15 aircraft of 48 Fighter Wing on the runway and see much of the associated infrastructure.

Snape Maltings Riverside Centre and Craft Shop. See page 46.

Suffolk Wildlife Park, Kessingland, Lowestoft NR33 7SL. Telephone: 01502 740291. 4¼ miles (7 km) south of Lowestoft, off A12.
Open daily.
Visitors will see African lions, cheetahs, zebra, giraffes, antelopes, monkeys and many more mammals and birds from around the world. Other attractions include animal feeding times, farmyard corner, flamingo walk, woodland walk and a large children's play area.

Valley Farm Camargue Horses and White Animal Collection, Valley Farm Riding and Driving Centre, Wickham Market IP13 9ND. Telephone: 01728 746916. Off B1078.
Open all year, Thursday to Tuesday.
This animal collection is best-known for its breeding herd of Camargue horses from southern France. There are also white animals such as the Arabian camel.

Winter Flora, Hall Farm, Weston, Beccles NR34 8TT. Telephone: 01502 713346. 3 miles (5 km) south of Beccles, off A145.
Open daily.
Dried flower arrangements and accessories are produced on this farm. Visitors can see work in progress in the workshop.

12
Famous people

Many of Suffolk's best-known inhabitants have been painters, poets or musicians.

Thomas Gainsborough (1727-88) grew up in the Suffolk countryside, then worked in London, Ipswich and Bath. His landscape paintings recall the influence of the Dutch masters, but also his rural childhood, as in 'Cornard Wood', near Sudbury (National Gallery, London). He was admired by royalty and his patrons came from a wide circle. The portraits they commissioned were often placed in idyllic landscapes, such as 'Queen Charlotte' and 'Mr and Mrs Andrews'.

George Crabbe (1754-1832) is Suffolk's most famous poet. The son of a fisherman, he was apprenticed to a surgeon and ordained as a minister. Samuel Johnson and Edmund Burke made him known through his poem *The Village*, published in 1783, a pithy story of smugglers, fishermen and paupers.

Another poet, **Robert Bloomfield** of Honington (1766-1823), famously observed contemporary farming life in *The Farmer's Boy,* which was published in 1800. It ran to 1500 lines describing the four seasons and by the seventh edition in 1883 some thirty thousand copies had been sold.

John Constable (1776-1837) attended the Royal Academy in 1799, then painted from his East Bergholt studio, capturing the essence of the Stour valley in a way not appreciated in his day; his work became far better known after an exhibition in 1888.

A later artist, **Harry Becker** (1865-1928), moved from Colchester to Wenhaston in 1913 to paint agricultural life beneath Suffolk skies, often working alongside farmers in the fields. The way of life was changing but his paintings were documentary and unsentimental and he hated selling them, buying them back whenever possible. They include 'Man Hedging' and 'Two Men Clearing the Banks of a Stream'.

Sir Alfred Munnings (1878-1959) was extrovert, colourful and probably the best painter of horses since Stubbs – a master of East Anglian landscape and its people. Born in Mendham and blinded in one eye at the age of twenty, he lived mainly in Dedham, Essex, and was fascinated by gypsies. In 1944, on the death of Lutyens, he was elected President of the Royal Academy and he was later knighted. His paintings include 'Travellers'.

Other painters having strong associations with Suffolk include **Philip Wilson Steer**, **John Moore**, **Leonard Squirrel**, **Thomas Churchyard** and, more recently, **Mary Potter**.

Benjamin Britten (1913-76), the composer, launched the Aldeburgh Festival of Music and the Arts in 1948 with Peter Pears and Eric Crozier. Since 1967 it has focused on Snape Maltings and achieved international status. Aldeburgh's seascapes and marshland brought Britten the musical inspiration for works like *Curlew River, Albert Herring* and *Peter Grimes,* based on Crabbe's *The Borough,* published in 1810. The Britten-Pears Library, Aldeburgh, is a working collection of manuscripts, books, music and recordings reflecting the interests and activities of Benjamin Britten and Peter Pears. Although the library is normally open to scholars and research students by appointment, during the Aldeburgh Festival in June open days are held for the general public. For further information telephone: 01728 452615.

Other Suffolk musicians have included the madrigal writer **John Wilbye** (page 98).

One of the best-known characters in local folklore is **Margaret Catchpole** (1773-1819), the lookout for the smuggler Will Laud. By day she worked for the Cobbold family in Ipswich and Laud was a ferryman. They were secret lovers, meeting when they could, and Margaret, disguised as a sailor, stole a horse to meet Will in London. She was arrested and imprisoned but escaped. Reunited, the couple travelled to Orford to emigrate to Holland. At the last minute, excisemen discovered them. Will was shot and Margaret, aged twenty-eight, was transported to Australia for life.

Amongst explorers and seafarers were **Thomas Cavendish**, second Englishman to sail round the world (page 27), and **Bartholomew Gosnold**, who named Cape Cod in 1602. **Richard Hakluyt** (c.1552-1616) was a pioneer geographer, who from Wetheringsett rectory in 1590 assembled a massive account of English voyages of discovery, and the plant collectors **William and Joseph Hooker** came from Halesworth (page 25).

Suffolk's success in agriculture was made possible by men like **Thomas Tusser** (died 1580) of Brantham, who published his *Hundred Goode Pointes of Husbandry* in 1557. **Arthur Young** (1741-1820), son of the rector of Bradfield Combust, continued this work. He inherited land which he found difficult to cultivate, so he travelled, surveyed, researched and published widely on the popular subject of agricultural improvement, becoming an expert on enclosure, reclamation and farm economics.

Thomas Wolsey (c.1475-1530), from Ipswich, took a degree from Oxford University aged fourteen and so was called the 'Boy Bachelor'. He became Archbishop of York in 1514, cardinal in 1515, Lord Chancellor, chief minister, godfather to Mary Tudor, a favourite of Henry VIII and a candidate for the papacy. He sought to endow a college in Ipswich; its completion would have brought immense prestige to the town, but he fell from favour with Henry VIII and the project foundered. A near contemporary was **Thomas Seckford** (page 53).

Elizabeth Garrett Anderson (1836-1917) was the daughter of Newson Garrett, who built Snape Maltings. She fought her way into the medical profession, to become the first female gynaecologist, founding the Elizabeth Garrett Anderson Hospital in London, the first hospital in Europe to be staffed by women doctors. In 1907 she became mayor of Aldeburgh and the first female mayor in England, her sister Millicent was a pioneer of women's suffrage.

Daniel Day was a chairmaker in Mendlesham who made distinctive Mendlesham or Dan Day chairs, resembling Windsor chairs. Dan Day's son is reputed to have worked for Sheraton c.1790 before returning to his father's workshop.

Robert Reyce (1555-1638), of Preston Hall, a noted antiquarian, wrote the *Breviary of Suffolk*. At Preston church he arranged the display in stained glass of 167 sets of heraldic arms dedicated to and putatively associated with Elizabeth I, ranging fancifully through history from Brutus onwards. A quarter of them remain.

13
Tourist information centres

Centres that are not open all year are denoted by an asterisk*.

Aldeburgh*: The Cinema, High Street, Aldeburgh IP15 5AU. Telephone: 01728 453637.
Beccles*: The Quay, Fen Lane, Beccles NR34 9BH. Telephone: 01502 713196.
Bury St Edmunds: 6 Angel Hill, Bury St Edmunds IP33 1UZ. Telephone: 01284 764667.
Felixstowe: Leisure Centre, Undercliff Road West, Felixstowe IP11 8AB. Telephone: 01394 276770.
Hadleigh: Toppesfield Hall, Hadleigh IP7 5DN. Telephone: 01473 823824.
Ipswich: St Stephen's Church, St Stephen's Lane, Ipswich IP1 1DP. Telephone: 01473 258070.
Lavenham*: Lady Street, Lavenham CO10 9RA. Telephone: 01787 248207.
Lowestoft: East Point Pavilion, Royal Plain, Lowestoft NR33 0AP. Telephone: 01502 523000.
Newmarket: 63 The Rookery, Newmarket CB8 8HT. Telephone: 01638 667200.
Southwold*: Town Hall, Market Place, Southwold IP18 6EF. Telephone: 01502 724729.
Stowmarket: Wilkes Way, Stowmarket IP14 1DE. Telephone: 01449 676800.
Sudbury*: Town Hall, Market Hill, Sudbury CO10 6TL. Telephone: 01787 881320.
Woodbridge: Station Buildings, Woodbridge. Telephone: 01394 444321. (Due to open 1996.)

14
Further reading

Alderton, D., and Booker, J. *The Batsford Guide to the Industrial Archaeology of East Anglia.* Batsford, 1980.

Bennet, Chloe. *Suffolk Artists 1750-1930.* Images Publications, 1991.

Betterton, Alec, and Dymond, David. *Lavenham Industrial Town.* Terence Dalton, 1989.

Bishop, Peter. *The History of Ipswich.* Unicorn Press, 1991.

Brown, C.; Haward, B.; and Kindred, R. *Dictionary of Architects of Suffolk Buildings, 1800-1914.* Suffolk Record Office, Ipswich, 1991.

Burke, John. *Suffolk.* Batsford, 1971.

Cautley, H. Munro. *Suffolk Churches.* Boydell, 1982.

Dymond, David, and Martin, Edward. *An Historical Atlas of Suffolk.* Suffolk County Council Planning Department, 1989.

Dymond, David, and Northeast, Peter. *A History of Suffolk.* Phillimore, 1985.

Evans, Angela Care. *The Sutton Hoo Ship Burial.* British Museum Publications, 1986.

Haining, Peter. *Maria Marten – The Murder in the Red Barn.* Richard Castell Publishing, 1992.

Haward, Birkin. *Nineteenth Century Suffolk Stained Glass.* Boydell, 1989.

Hussey, Frank. *Suffolk Invasion.* Terence Dalton, 1983.

Innes, Hammond. *Hammond Innes' East Anglia.* Hodder & Stoughton, 1986.

James, M. R. *Suffolk and Norfolk.* Alastair Press, 1987.

Jebb, Miles. *Suffolk.* Random House/Pimlico, 1995.

Jesty, Chris. *East Anglian Town Trails.* Robert Hale, 1989.

Jobson, Alan. *The Illustrated Portrait of Suffolk.* Robert Hale, 1987.

Kent, Peter. *Fortifications of East Anglia.* Terence Dalton, 1988.

Kinsey, Gordon. *Orfordness Secret Site.* Terence Dalton, 1981.

Malster, Robert. *Lowestoft East Coast Port.* Terence Dalton, 1982.

Mitchels, Mark and Elizabeth. *Suffolk: A Portrait in Colour.* Countryside Books, 1993.

Moore, Derek. *Watching Wildlife in Suffolk.* Suffolk Wildlife Trust, 1994.

Perring, Franklyn. *A Guide to the Nature Reserves of Eastern England.* Macmillan, 1991.

Pevsner, Nikolaus. *The Buildings of England: Suffolk.* Penguin, 1974.

Phelps, Humphrey. *Suffolk of a Hundred Years Ago.* Allan Sutton, 1992.

Pratt, Jean and Geoffrey. *Pub Walks in Suffolk.* Countryside Books, 1994.

Reyce, Robert. *Breviary of Suffolk, or a Plaine and Familier Description of the Country.* 1603.

Sandon, Eric. *Suffolk Houses, A Study of Domestic Architecture.* Antique Collectors Club, 1993.

Scarfe, Norman. *Suffolk in the Middle Ages.* Boydell, 1985.

Scarfe, Norman. *The Suffolk Landscape.* Alastair Press, 1987.

Scarfe, Norman. *The Suffolk Guide.* Alastair Press, 1988.

Simper, Robin. *The Suffolk Sandlings.* East Anglian Magazine Publishing, 1986.

Simper, Robin. *Rivers Alde, Ore and Blyth.* Creekside Publishing, 1994.

Simpson, Francis W. *Simpson's Flora of Suffolk.* Suffolk Naturalists' Society, 1982.

Smith, Graham. *Suffolk Airfields in the Second World War.* Countryside Books, 1995.

Suffolk Historic Churches Trust. *Suffolk Churches: A Pocket Guide.* Suffolk Historic Churches Trust, 1976.

Timpson, John. *Timpson's Travels in East Anglia.* Heinemann, 1990.

Walpole, Josephine. *Suffolk Lives.* Richard Castell Publishing, 1993.

Whitehead, R. A. *The Beloved Coast and Suffolk Sandlings.* Terence Dalton, 1991.

Index

Page numbers in italic refer to illustrations.